Lists for $75.00
- Morrison's; Western Americana
  catalogue prices, vol.8 - 1994

11-00

P9-CMV-135

(out of print)

70

BOSQUE REDONDO

An American Concentration Camp

An American Concentration Camp

Bosque Redondo

by

Lynn R. Bailey

Socio-Technical Books . . . 1970 . . . Pasadena, California

To

R. L. H. and K. D. B.

Contents

Illustrations

ACKNOWLEDGMENT

I wish to gratefully acknowledge the wonderful cooperation of the personnel of the Army and Navy Branch, the Cartographic, and the Audio Visual Branches of the National Archives, Washington, D.C. Archaeologists David Brugge and Lee Correll have likewise been helpful in making available copies of the Historical Findings for the Navajo Tribal Land Claims cases.

L. R. BAILEY

BOSQUE REDONDO

An American Concentration Camp

Introduction

FOR NEARLY five years — from 1863 to 1868 — Fort Sumner was the concentration camp for the majority of Navajo Indians, rounded up by an intensive military campaign conducted by General James Carleton and Colonel Christopher "Kit" Carson. On forty square miles surrounding Bosque Redondo, a clump of cottonwoods on the banks of the Rio Pecos, in east-central New Mexico, nearly 9,000 Indians grubbed out a meager subsistence from alkali impregnated soil, lived by army doctrine, or died of dysentary induced by brackish water, and syphilis contracted from the garrison. Never in the lives of a people had a more traumatic moment existed. In fact, so traumatic was this event in Navajo life, that tribesmen would reckon all future events from the day of release — as if the tribe had been reborn and all earlier happenings were of little consequence.

Much has been written of this period in Navajo history known to Anglo-Americans as the "Long Walk," or Bosque Redondo, and to the Indians as *Hwelte*. Statements are numerous and varied as to the effectiveness of Carson's campaign; of the rigors of the movement of Indians from their traditional homeland to their new reservation at Bosque Redondo; and of the treatment received from army overseers during their period of incarceration. Anthropologists state that this was a period of "intense directed change," during which time traits of an alien culture were forced upon the tribe. Historians — taking the stand now in vogue — state that the Navajo menace was destined to be removed, for it stood in the path of Anglo-American expansion. Both views are right, but both fail to graphically portray the consequences of the situation. For the Indian this was a period of intense hardship and uncertainty. Every enemy of the Navajos had been unleashed, and it often seemed as if no escape was possible. The soldiers, their Ute, Pueblo, and New Mexican allies were unrelenting. They struck during summer, fall, and winter — slaughtering herds, burning planting grounds, and destroying orchards. Every strata of Navajo society felt this war, and there was no escape this time, for the order was: "All must go to Bosque Redondo." The stresses endured by the Navajos during this period will never be fully understood, for it is nearly impossible for whitemen to fathom the effects on personality and culture which this upheaval must surely have had.

The term *stress* has often defied definition — and for that very reason, stress and its related concepts have been largely overlooked by historians and anthropologists. But this has not been the case with other fields of science. In the literature of medicine, sociology and psychology are found two familiar terms — stimulus and trauma — both connoting factors contributing to the physical upheaval of the individual, as well as to the disintegration of social and cultural units. In all three cases the terms stimulus, trauma, and stress, are used in a rather vague, unspecific way, not primarily for the intrinsic meaning they carry, but because they enable the social scientist and the medical man to think with greater clarity and verbal distinctness about extremely important reaction processes.

Stress, therefore, is a rather broad conceptual term. It can be compared to a tennis racket, with which we can bat about, like tennis balls, some concepts which are concerned with definable reaction processes. Because of this broad and seemingly all encompassing framework, the concept of stress can indeed be a useful tool. When linked with detailed historical evidence, as well as to ethnological data, it can produce an amazingly clear picture of conditions and reactions of peoples torn by force from their traditional environment, and whose daily lives and futures rest solely upon the dictates of aliens.

Studies conducted during the Japanese Relocation Program of World War II — a situation not at all dissimilar to the Navajo internment — enlarged and developed the conceptual framework of stress. Alexander H. Leighton, a sociologist, working among the Neis at Poston, Arizona, closely observed the trauma of prison camp conditions; and in a subsequent book, *The Governing of Men,* specifically outlined the factors which are so disturbing to the emotions and thoughts of people in confinement:

1. Threats to life and health
2. Discomfort from pain, heat, cold, dampness, fatigue and poor food
3. Loss of means of subsistence and property
4. Restriction of movement
5. Isolation
6. Threats to family members and friends

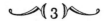

7. Rejection, dislike and ridicule from other people
8. Capricious and unpredictable behavior on the part of those in authority upon whom the welfare of the group depends

At initial glance these factors appear to be nothing more than an unwarranted statement of the obvious. Indeed, this would be true, were it not for the rarity with which the obvious is acted upon during crucial times. As Leighton points out, "The people who actually feel the ill effects of stress are, of course, aware of them, but others at the moment, though in a position to see plainly, can be blind to a degree that often seems incredible in later perspectives."

Looking in depth at these specific types of stresses and projecting them to conditions at Bosque Redondo, we are enabled to better understand the state of upheaval which the Navajo Indians experienced. From the historical record and from ethnology the basic types of stress are quickly discerned for that period in Navajo history.

It was the threat of life and subsistence which brought these Indians into Forts Canby and Wingate during the winter of 1863-64. Kit Carson, knowing well the Indian character and economic structure, systematically destroyed every Navajo planting ground, and then unleashed every enemy known to the Diné — the Utes, Puebloans, and the New Mexicans. With the onset of freezing weather, the consequences were obvious.

Other types of stress, such as physical discomfort and disruption of family and social units, hung like a double-edged sword over the Navajos at Fort Sumner. Completely destitute of clothing, shelter, and food, they indeed suffered greatly, both during the "Long Walk" to, and at Bosque Redondo. The intensive military control which the army superimposed upon the aboriginal form of government completely wiped away every vestige of tribal organization and planted the seeds for the development of the present-day tribal council.

However, other types of stress, not so clearly understood in previous studies, rear their head as the situation at Bosque Redondo is probed. The basic and innate fear of isolation, of living far removed from a country which was familiar and sacred, was without a doubt, extremely alarming to the Navajos. Unlike many tribes, these Indians were never great travelers and it has been noted that Navajos are not even familiar with areas in their own homeland, fifty miles distant. When two-thirds of the tribe was gathered up and removed some 400 miles to a land as stark as the biblical wilderness, the symptoms of intense aggression and withdrawal, which were manifested by Navajos at the time, can be more easily understood. The capricious management of the reservation by the military; their strict surveillance of the Indians, and at times inhuman dictates; as well as their continual battle with the Office of Indian Affairs, produced in the Navajos a feeling of being no more than pawns in a greater power struggle.

All of these stresses — as simple as they may appear — were present during the Navajo removal of 1863-64 and their incarceration at Bosque Redondo; and all produced behavior within the individual and the group which was not recognized by the military at the time. In fact, for a century these disruptive elements have been skirted by writers, historians, and anthropologists. Dramatic portrayals of Carson's sweep through Cañon de Chelly, of the Long Walk, and of the Fort

Sumner reservation exist. But few writers have attempted to probe Navajo reactions to these situations.

It is for those reasons that this book was undertaken. Although all secondary writings pertaining to the Long Walk and the Bosque Redondo period have been scanned, great reliance has been put upon original correspondence of the military and the Office of Indian Affairs, now located in the National Archives, in Washington, D.C. This has been done in order to ferret out the truths relating to the period of Navajo incarceration, and to more accurately set the stage and bring forth the actors in a drama which is still fresh in the minds of a native people, as one of their most traumatic periods.

Chapter One

WHEN THE Navajo Indians entered the Southwest their culture was simple. They came like the Paiutes, as hunters and gatherers. From the sedentary Puebloans, these people from the north, grasped a rudimentary knowledge of agriculture, that enabled them to better exploit an environment which was brutally harsh and precarious. With the arrival of the Spanish in the Rio Grande Valley, during the 16th century came sheep and horses, as well as an associated complex of traits, which the receptive Navajos quickly adopted to their culture. Livestock revolutionized Navajo economics. The horse brought mobility and tribal expansion; and sheep and their products brought wealth, status, and trading relationships. Within a relatively short span of time, the Navajos had become an agricultural-pastoral society, and with that change had come a set of new goals for both the individual and the group. A new system of social stratification and prestige emerged.

With the transition from the ill-defined *"Apache de Najabo"* to *"Nacion de Navajo"* began the long years of reciprocal encroachments, transgressions, and conflicts of economic interests between the Navajos and their Spanish-speaking neighbors. By 1700 the population drift which had brought these Indians into the Southwest had ceased, and they were settled upon lands which to this day they claim. From that date the Navajo people became a tribal entity in the administrative eyes of first Spain, and then the subsequent nations of Mexico and the United States.

In reality, however, political solidarity among the Navajo is of very recent origin, beginning in 1927 with the development, by the Bureau of Indian Affairs, of local community organizations and other artificial political mechanisms. What three governments could not, and would not understand, was that the Navajo people were not organized as a "Nation" in the strict sense of the word. As Kluckhohn and Leighton point out, tribal feelings rest upon "a common language; a common designation for themselves as The People [Diné] as distinct from all others; a cultural heritage which is, *in general,* the same; and a territory with a certain topographical unity." The only sense of community which these people possessed was based upon the existence of an exogamous clan system which held together tribal segments dispersed over a broad geographical area.

These clans were further organized into groupings which were not localized at all, and which acted to extend clan ties throughout the entire tribe. Although these "bands" were composed of related members, and had home areas, they nevertheless moved about Navajo country for economic, social, and religious purposes. These bands were further organized in an hierarchical manner, based primarily upon wealth and status, determined to a large extent by the possession of livestock. On the lowest level were the *pobres,* who possessed but few animals. Their attempts to climb the Navajo social ladder by acquisition of livestock brought continual conflict to the tribe as a whole, and to themselves the appropriate label of *ladrones,* or thieves. The *pobres* could be compared to the "hawks" of present-day Anglo-American society, for they desired a state of war which afforded them ample opportunity for self-enrichment. At the other extreme of band organization were the influential and wealthy. It was from the ranks of the *ricos* that band leaders originated — and it were they who had the most to loose during time of strife. For the most part, the *ricos* were the "doves" of the Navajo people, for they desired to maintain equilibrium and peace. Outside the bands, however, the power of these leaders greatly diminished.

Imbued with a rigid political viewpoint, the whiteman could not see the weakness inherent in the Navajo social and political structure. A single leader, responsible for the actions of all tribal members, was invariable sought. And when such a person was not found, one was created. The practice of selecting an influential Indian, presenting him with a medal and staff of office, began with the Spanish and was perpetuated by subsequent governments.

The lack of political solidarity of these Indians, and the desire for wealth and status by the poorer elements of the tribe, combined with the insatiable desire for land on the part of the whiteman, to create more than 150 years of chaos throughout the Southwest. Between 1700 and 1863 nineteen separate treaties were enacted between the Navajos and the whiteman—as the latter slyly endeavored to play power politics in an ever-ending attempt to gain more and more territory. The more than forty government-sanctioned military campaigns into Navajo country, as well as hundreds of private

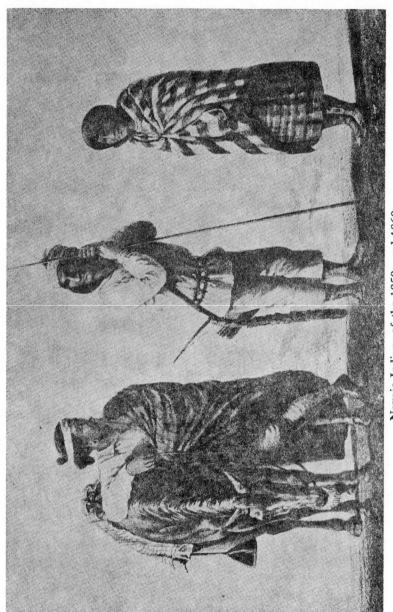

Navajo Indians of the 1850s and 1860s

punitive expeditions, attest to the success of these political maneuverings. Only by the most drastic measures would this unfortunate combination of administrative shortsightedness, and the conflicts of economic and cultural interests, be overcome. Only by the forced removal of two-thirds of the Navajo people from their traditional homeland would more than 150 years of conflict be brought to a halt.

This removal — while projected as early as the mid-1700s — was slow in coming. Weak politically and militarily, Mexico was unable to accomplish anything but send out abortive campaigns, and appease tribal leaders during times of peace. And much the same condition was carried over into the Anglo-American period, following the 1846 takeover of New Mexico. For nearly twenty years, one punitive expedition followed another against the tribe. But the use of infantry to chase mounted Indians came to nought. United States firepower was just too weak to intimidate the Navajo in those early years. It would, in fact, take the marshalling of military strength for a far greater conflict to set the stage for the complete subjection of the Navajos.

In New Mexico — as elsewhere across the nation — the effects of succession were immediately apparent and hard felt during the early months of 1861. Army officers by scores resigned their commissions to take up the cause of their native states and beloved South. Colonel Thomas T. Fauntleroy, the land speculating Department Commander, resigned on March 25. His successor, Colonel William Wing Loring, a dashing cavalry officer who would one day become a soldier of fortune in the Near East, followed suit sixty days later. And Major Henry Hopkins Sibley, an inventive alcoholic and more than able tactician when sober, departed the territory after prophetically telling the soldiers at Fort Fillmore: "Boys, if you only knew it, I am the worst enemy you have!"

Command of the United States Army in New Mexico fell to the next senior officer — Edward R. S. Canby. This mild mannered, plain appearing officer had seen service in New Mexico but a short time, having been transferred from Fort Garland, Colorado, at the head of a column of seven companies to subdue the Navajos during the fall of 1860. Regardless of his short tour of duty in New Mexico, years of military experience qualified Canby as a competent field commander. Upon graduation from West Point in 1839, he served in Florida against the Seminoles; had been with General Scott in Mexico, and knew firsthand the rigors of frontier duty.

By a series of quick sorties through Indian country, Canby intimidated the Navajos; and by end of February 1861 he had drawn up a peace with the tribe, and was attempting to strengthen it by isolating the Navajos from their traditional enemies, the New Mexicans. Colonel Canby, however, was destined never to have the opportunity to take the measures he deemed necessary for securement of a permanent peace with the Indians. To the east and south of New Mexico another conflict of far greater magnitude was gathering. With election of Abraham Lincoln to the presidency the question of Negro slavery and state's rights was brought once and for all to a head.

The resignation of the elite of the army left the defense of the Far West in shambles. The task of reorganizing the scattered troops under Canby's command would be exceedingly difficult, if not impossible. The army in New Mexico was struck by one of the wost epidemics of demoralization in its history. By summer of 1861 the weak and scattered companies found themselves with pay half a year in arrears; and severe droughts, which struck New Mexico for eighteen months, had left the cavalry with few serviceable mounts. The Indians, sensing the weakened condition of the military, ran riot. Mescaleros to the south, and their cousins the Chiricahua Apaches pillaged deep into Mexico — causing that government to lodge numerous protestations against the inability of the United States to live up to the stipulations of the Treaty of Guadalupe Hildalgo. To the north and west, Navajos incited by an age-old conflict with New Mexicans and by their own drive for status through acquisition of livestock, repeatedly struck the sheep ranchers along the Rio Puerco and the upper Rio Grande, driving off more than 200,000 sheep and horses, causing a frantic clamor from stockmen for more military protection.

While Canby feverishly worked to curb the disintegration of New Mexico's defenses and to affect some measure of security from Indian incursions, Henry Hopkins Sibley was before President Jefferson Davis outlining a grandiose scheme for the conquest of the Desert Southwest.

With a commission of brigadier general in the Confederate Army, Sibley by June 1861 was on his way back to Texas with Jefferson Davis' authorization to undertake the conquest of New Mexico. By year's end, 3500 Texans of "the best that ever threw a leg over a horse or that had ever sworn allegiance to any cause" were on their way northward, up the Rio Grande Valley. The words Sibley uttered that day at Fort Fillmore had become a reality.

News of Sibley's movements added impetus to Canby's work. From the War Department he secured authority to raise four regiments of New Mexican volunteers; and by end of September, Canby had fourteen ill-equipped companies, on enlistments as short as six months. This number fell far short of the necessary quota to fill out four units. However, two regiments could be mustered — and the First and Second New Mexico Volunteers were created.

To lead these regiments, Canby picked men whom he knew commanded respect, and whose loyalty to the Union was beyond question. Christopher "Kit" Carson, although illiterate, was a veteran of Rocky Mountain fur trade, an explorer and Indian fighter of high repute, and more recently Ute Indian Agent — an excellent choice for commander of the First Regiment, Canby felt. An almost equally illustrious New Mexican was given command of the Second Regiment. As a man of unquestioned Union sympathies, an able administrator, publisher and politician from Santa Fe, Miguel Pino would also prove an excellent field officer, although his tour of duty would be short, lasting until the expulsion of the Confederates from the territory. José Francisco Chavez, American educated step-son of New Mexico's Governor, Henry Connelly, would be placed second in command to Carson.

Two regiments were hardly enough to repulse a Confederate invasion, let alone police nearly 100,000 Indians spread over what is today Arizona and New Mexico. In the manner of all regular army officers, Canby doubted the ability of volunteer troops, and he beseeched the War Department for more contingents of regulars. Canby's requests were met with the notification that the meager force of regulars under his command would soon be transferred elsewhere. In desperation he enlisted the aid of Governor William Gilpin, of Colorado, who consented to rush a volunteer force southward.

While awaiting reinforcements, Canby shifted his troops, withdrawing units from isolated posts such as Fort Fauntleroy (now renamed Fort Lyon for obvious reasons) and concentrated them at more strategic points. Forts Fillmore, Stanton, and Craig — posts that would feel the brunt of Texas invasion — were strengthened.

The Confederate tide was strong and rapid. It swept up the Rio Grande during the summer and fall of 1861, engulfing Fort Fillmore, causing the abandonment of Fort Stanton; and paralyzing the territory's nerve centers of Albuquerque and Santa Fe. Brigadier General Henry Hopkins Sibley, however, was never to realize his dream of conquest. Intemperance dulled and slowed the brilliance of his strategy, and Colorado Volunteers led by Colonel John B. Slough, accidently discovered the Texans' supply train at Glorieta Pass in February 1862.

Sibley's invasion of New Mexico had failed ignominiously. But the conquest of the upper Rio Grande had never been the primary objective of the Confederacy — as Sibley had so fervently pointed out in Richmond. In reality, the gold fields and seaports of the Pacific Coast were the particular and immediate objective. Southern sympathies had always run high in California, and the Confederate secret organization, the Knights of the Golden Circle, flourished throughout the state — primarily in the south. Geographically isolated by thousands of miles of desert and mountains, California was viewed by pro-Southern advocates as a potential "Republic of the Pacific."

With outbreak of war, this state of condition was quite naturally brought to the forefront. In August 1861, commanding officer of the Department of the Pacific, Brigadier General Edwin Vose Sumner, advised that secessionists were "energetically at work" all over the state, and generally there was "a deep and abiding hatred" of the federal government. At least 20,000 Southern sympathizers could create havoc, Sumner warned, if organized and trained.

Northern Mexico was also a tempting morsel to expanionists and states-righters. Ever since the early 1850s it had been more than apparent that the South had clear intentions of expanding into Mexico, and perhaps even as far as Cuba. The long Mexican coast line defied blockade, and its boundless natural resources would stoke the Southern war machine. But what was more immediately important, was that *politicos* in the border states of Sonora, Chihuahua, Tamaulipas, Nuevo Leon, and Coahuila, were openly hostile to the central government of President Juarez — offering a moment ripe for Confederate intervention.

The dream of mastery of the Southwest was more than lifesize in the minds of Confederate leaders. Early in January 1862 the Confederate Congress at Richmond approved the creation of the "Territory of Arizona;" and to back up this congressional act, a force of "Rangers" had been dispatched to Tucson, early in Sibley's campaign.

To Union military men, the situation was precarious to say the least. Overland communications had been interrupted and the thought of Confederate expansion into Mexico was unnerving. It was imperative, therefore, that this threat be countered; and Secretary of War Simon Cameron moved

swiftly. Governor of California, John G. Downey, was authorized to raise one regiment of infantry and five companies of
cavalry, and instructions were given Sumner to begin immediately preparing an expedition which would embark at San
Francisco for Mazatlan, Sinoloa, and travel overland to New
Mexico and Texas. Machinations by secessionist elements attempting to seize control of California, and the transfer of
Sumner to the eastern theater of war altered this plan.

The new Department Commander, General George G.
Wright, formulating an alternate plan, sought the Adjutant
General's permission to move the recently organized California Volunteers south and eastward to prevent secessionists
from fleeing California, and at the same time, march into Arizona and New Mexico to secure military posts along the
Rio Grande, thus permanently restoring overland communications.

By mid-December 1861 Wright's plan had been approved
by both the Adjutant General and Major General George B.
McClellan, commanding Union Armies. At Wright's sugges-
tion, Colonel James Henry Carleton, a veteran Dragoon, was
appointed commander of the "California Column" — as these
troops would be called.

An iron-willed disciplinarian, James H. Carleton was an
ideal choice for the task that lay ahead. He was a relatively
young man — only forty-seven years of age; and his New
England upbringing assured unquestioned loyalty to the Union, at a time when loyalties were being cast aside like ill-fit-
ting clothes.

Unlike many fellow army officers, James Carleton gained
his army commission through the back door. He was not a
West Point graduate, and perhaps the army had not even

General James H. Carleton
The austere and inflexible founder of Fort Sumner and promoter of the
Bosque Redondo experiment.   (*Courtesy Huntington Library*)

been his first love. He desired a literary career far above all else prior to entering the service. In fact, he had sought the aid of Charles Dickens in 1833, only to be rebuffed by the great social critic, and told to seek his inspiration — like so many of his peers—in the scenes of the American frontier. It was this desire that led the young man from Maine into military service.

Enlisting during the boundary conflict with Canada, Carleton was commissioned a lieutenant of Maine militia in August 1838. His conduct, and qualities of organization and leadership immediately attracted the attention of his superiors, and his military career was assured. In October of the following year he applied for, and was accepted, for training in the elite of United States armed forces, the recently organized First Dragoons.

For over a year Carleton labored at the Cavalry School, Carlisle, Pennsylvania. Under the strict discipline of Captain Edwin Vose Sumner, cavalry drill, care of horses and equipment, as well as military etiquette was pounded home. The five years which followed this rigorous training, gave Carleton every chance to realize his literary aspirations. His tour of duty on the Great Plains during 1844-45 furnished material and inspiration for the writing of his *Log Books*. But it was the appointment as Assistant Commissary of Subsistence at Fort Leavenworth in 1842, which gave Carleton the practical knowledge so beneficial for the organization of his California troops twenty years later.

The outbreak of the Mexican War broadened James Carleton's horizons. As aide-de-camp to General John E. Wool, he participated in the Battle of Buena Vista, and later produced the first chronicle of the conflict. Emerging from the

Mexican War as a major, Carleton was transferred to New Mexico in 1851, with the command of his Dragoon instructor, Colonel Edwin V. Sumner.

For the next few years Carleton chased Apaches with Kit Carson and conducted several reconnaissances of east-central New Mexico, both of which took him over ground which he would later hinge his career upon, and which would forever be associated with him.

Carleton's record as a Dragoon and cavalry tactician, as well as his writing skills drew the attention of Secretary of War Jefferson Davis, who in 1856 was organizing a commission to study the tactics of European armies, then fighting in the Crimea. Major Carleton was assigned the study of the Russian Cossacks. It was his observations of European videttes that shaped Carleton's California troops in 1861.

A strict disciplinarian like his teacher, E. V. Sumner, James Carleton drilled and whipped into shape his 2500 men. The rigors of desert campaigns demanded unflinching courage, and the ability to manage animal and weapons like veterans.

Although Carleton was a romantic dreamer, he had that rare gift for transferring fantasies into reality. From his years of frontier service, he quickly grasped the drama inherent in this venture. Spectacular marches over the most desolate region of North America and an opportunity "to strike a blow for the old flag" was at hand. Nothing must be overlooked in the preparation of this campaign. From one end of the state to the other his quartermasters rummaged. Saddles, ammunition, horses, bridles, Indian goods, haversacks and knapsacks, commissary supplies, rifles and revolvers and sabers — everything to equip a sizeable contingent of troops, and more, was concentrated at Fort Yuma on the Colorado River. To all, Carleton lent his personal scrutiny.

Late in March 1862 the first units moved out of Fort Yuma under command of Joseph R. West, bound for Tucson. The main body of troops left May 16. The march of Carleton's California Column is history. In Tucson and elsewhere, his iron hand fell heavily on Southern sympathizers — both real and imaginery; and upon arrival in the Mesilla Valley he minced few words in ordering "all inhabitants along the Rio Grande southward from the Jornada del Muerto to Fort Bliss" to repair their dwellings, and clean up their streets. No breach of loyalty to the Union would be permitted.

For ten long months Carleton's California Column had been on the march. Although widely heralded, these troops participated but little in the Civil War as fought in the far Southwest. While the California troops were toiling over the desert, Canby with his rag-tailed New Mexicans, and help from volunteer forces in Colorado, dulled the Confederate bid for mastery and finally sent Sibley reeling southward in defeat, leaving behind his baggage, artillery, and guidons.

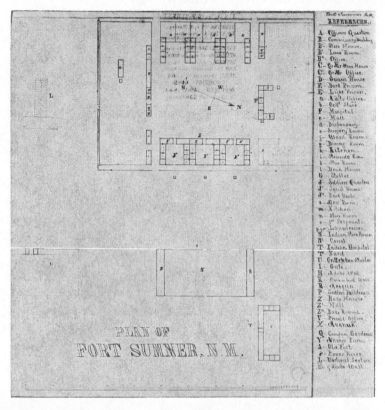

This plan of Fort Sumner, approved by James H. Carleton, provided for rigidly built adobe officers quarters, company barracks, Indian hospital and storage rooms, as well as oversized quartermaster and commissary facilities which would accommodate the produce from the Indian and government farms at Bosque Redondo.

(Courtesy National Archives)

Chapter Two

FALL OF 1862 came suddenly to the Rio Grande Valley, the first frosts changing the cottonwoods from verdant green to gold. In Santa Fe and Albuquerque people talked of an early winter; of the security which the newly arrived California troops would give the territory; and of the profits they would surely make from trade with the military.

Since his arrival in Santa Fe, early in September, the asture James Carleton had maintained discipline among his troops by keeping them busy with civic repairs and duties, while he and his staff plotted strategy and endeavored to find ways of strengthening the territory's defenses. He had not been in New Mexico since 1854, and it was imparative that he was brought abreast of not only military matters, but of the economic conditions of the territory as well. Public officials, newspaper men, ranchers, miners, and contractors of every ilk, flowed in and out of his offices. From all Carleton gathered information. But it was to Canby that he paid the utmost attention.

In briefings from his commander, Carleton learned of the havoc which the Indians were wreaking. The Apaches, particularly the Mescaleros and the Gilas, were rampaging to the south and west, and bitter were the complaints from Mexico. To the north and west, the Navajos were decimating New Mexican livestock. Canby's campaign of 1860-61 against that tribe had failed miserably, and itinerant volunteer companies, raised to protect frontier settlements, only infuriated the Indians. So out of hand had the issue between Navajos and whitemen become that Canby firmly believed that there was little alternative between complete annihilation of the Indians or removing and colonizing them "at points so removed from the settlements as to isolate them entirely from the inhabitants of the territory."

Canby wasted few words in letting Carleton know what the situation was, and in suggesting that any Indian removal could be performed most admirably by volunteer troops — for their hatred of the red man was well known. In tracking Indians the New Mexicans had few peers.

With the transfer of Canby to Washington, Carleton assumed the commandership of the Territory of New Mexico, and with it the rank of brigadier general. This was the time which would test the general's genius — and Carleton knew it. He weighed Canby's advise and added his own touches.

Nearly ten years had passed since Carleton had seen New Mexican trailers and scouts in action. But the memory of their effectiveness during the campaign against the Jicarilla Apaches was still fresh in the general's mind. Unlike Canby, Carleton did not mistrust militia and native auxiliaries. From his study of Russian Cossacks, he knew how valuable native contingents could be, if trained properly and given incentive, as well as freedom of movement.

He would utilize New Mexicans in this Indian war, and his field commanders would be the best Indian fighters procura-

ble. To punish and control the Mescaleros, he ordered Colonel
Christopher Carson, with five companies of the First New
Mexico Volunteers, to re-occupy Fort Stanton in the heart of
Apache country. To support Carson's movements, his Cali-
fornia troops were detailed to cooperate — "yet to be inde-
pendent . . ."

The Apaches would be caught in a pincer movement. On
October 11 Carleton requested Colonel Joseph R. West, Commandant of the recently established District of Arizona, to
dispatch two companies of First Cavalry, California Volunteers, with twenty Mexican guides, to move by way of Dog
Cañon and operate to the east and southeast of Mescalero
haunts. At the same time, other companies of the same regiment, guided by "first-rate" Pueblo Indians and Mexicans,
would proceed to the north of the Apaches. Company commanders were given strict orders not to hold talks with the
Indians — as this would be a war of extermination. "The men
are to be slain whenever and wherever they can be found,"
Carleton emphatically ordered. "The women and children
may be taken prisoners . . ., they are not to be killed."

Five months later the Mescaleros had been humbled. Three
hundred and fifty had surrendered and the remainder had
fled across the border into Mexico, or joined Gila Apaches in
the White Mountains. On February 1, 1863, Brigadier General James Carleton reported to Washington that "the Mescalero Apaches had been completely subdued."

Anticipating the results of his campaign, Carleton had begun planning the establishment of a post to receive and watch
over the snared Apaches. The grasslands bordering the Pecos
River Valley, below Anton Chico to the old rendezvous point
at Bosque Redondo, had impressed Carleton in 1853-54. The

This view, taken in late 1862, shows the temporary log and sod dwellings at Bosque Redondo that would become Fort Sumner. These miserable huts would be rapidly replaced by sturdy adobe buildings as specified by the Quartermaster Department plans on page 22. (*Courtesy National Archives*)

area was far removed from centers of population, and was traversed only by marauding Indians and itinerant traders. No better place could be found in all of New Mexico for an Indian reservation; and on November 4, 1862 Carleton issued Special Orders Number 193:

> A board of officers, to consist of Lieutenant Colonel Dodd, 2d Colorado Volunteers, Surgeon James M. McNulty, 1st Infantry California Volunteers, and First Lieutenant Cyrus H. DeForrest, 2nd Colorado Volunteers, will convene at Bosque Redondo, on the Pecos River, New Mexico, on the 15th of November, 1862, or as soon thereafter as practicable and proceed to select the exact site of Fort Sumner, the new post recently ordered to be established.

One month later the board of officers had accomplished their task; they had carefully and dispassionately inspected that portion of the Pecos River Valley known as Bosque Redondo. For fourteen miles, above and below the clump of cottonwoods which named the site, the terrain was scanned and measured. When the board submitted its report to Carleton, however, there was little in it to please the general.

The only advantage to selecting Bosque Redondo as site for Fort Sumner was that much of the land was high, and not subject to flooding, and commanded a view for "two or three miles in every direction." Water and fuel were close at hand, and the board considered the grazing in the area adequate.

Bosque Redondo, however, was remote from Fort Union, the quartermaster depot for the Department of New Mexico. It would be necessary to transport building supplies a great distance and at high costs. The waters of the stream were tested by the medical officer, and found to contain "much unhealthy mineral matter;" and a large part of the surrounding valley, which would be the site of the projected Indian reservation, was subject to inundation by spring floods.

"In view of the disadvantages of the location," the board of inspection, ". . . respectfully recommend that the junction of the Agua Negra and Pecos Rivers, be selected as the site of Fort Sumner, for the following reasons: The supply of good timber for building and firewood is convenient to the site. The water is pure and abundant; the grazing is very fine. None of the neighboring country is subject to overflow. . . ."

It is hard to visualize what Carleton's reactions must have been, when handed this report. In reality, he had selected these officers not to choose the site for Fort Sumner, but to approve his choice. The general's mind had been made up even before the board of officers arrived on the Pecos River. Fort Sumner would be situated at Bosque Redondo in east-central New Mexico, 165 miles from Santa Fe. Carleton had been over the ground in 1853 and again in 1854 — and both times he had considered the area of strategic importance. The Pecos, rising in the mountains near Santa Fe, appeared to be of sufficient volume to supply the needs of both military garrison and the contemplated Indian reservation.

Located in a large oblong valley, having the river as its western boundary, Fort Sumner would be perfectly situated for settlement of one of the most troublesome of tribes. To the east and south rose a low mesa which extended and blended into the Staked Plain. The country to the north and west was open for many miles, and the nearest settlement was fifty miles away. Placed at Bosque Redondo, Fort Sumner would stand as a barrier to the marauding Comanches and Kiowas, who had long used the area as a rendezvous for organization of raids into Mexico. Establish the post at Bosque Redondo, and the Mescalero Apaches, Comanches, Kiowas, and other Plains and Mountain tribes would forever be blocked in their devastating raids to the south. Carleton would not be vetoed by a board of inexperienced officers.

While the Mescalero Apaches were being driven to their "brutal senses," Carleton was carefully and metaphorically working out his policy relative to the management of the Navajo problem. By application of force-of-arms, he would gather this tribe together "little by little, on a reservation, away from their haunts and hills, and hiding-places of their country." Benevolently Carleton thought. His policy would be kind; young Navajos would be taught to read and write, the truths of Christianity, and the arts of peace, would be instilled in these Indians. "Soon they would acquire new habits, new ideas, new modes of life." The old and more stubborn tribesmen would die off, to be replaced by Carleton's educated and acculturated young. The turmoil which Navajos had caused would be a thing of the past. The prose Carleton heaped upon the War Department in an effort to convince it of his humanitarian intentions were voluminous.

The commandant of the Department of New Mexico, however, may very well have had other reasons for commencing a campaign not only against the Navajos, but all other Indians as well. Pay of regular army officers was notoriously low in those days, and many men turned to other ventures to augment their military pitance. Some like John Cremony and John G. Bourke would turn to writing, and in so doing chronicle well the frontier army. Others would turn to commercial ventures, not the least of which was mining. Nearly all the officers stationed along the Mexican border, near Tucson, during the 1850s were involved in mining speculation of one form or another. The now-Confederate General, Richard S. Ewell was constantly on the lookout for rich ore outcrops while serving a tour of duty in the Far West. Sylvester Mowry, when not bedding with a squaw or white girl, was promoting mining; and he eventually became owner of a large silver-lead producing property in the Patagonia Mountains of southern Arizona. Close by, Samuel P. Hientzelman, in partnership with others, ran the Cerro Colorado mines. And like his fellow commanding officers — Carleton desired to advance the economic interests of the area through the development of mineral resources.

Although Navajo country possessed little actual mineral wealth, still it had not been explored sufficiently at that time to ascertain the fact. Carleton had every reason to hope for active mining operations, once the Navajos had been removed. His letters to the Adjutant General, the Commander-in-Chief of the Army, and the Secretary of War, outlined grandiose schemes for the advancement of mineral exploration. "There is every evidence," wrote the general, "that a country as rich if not richer in mineral wealth than California, extends from the Rio Grande, northwestwardly, all the way across Washoe."

In the eyes of James Carleton the United States Army was the means of extending economic advancement and civilization; and all that stood in the way — whether man or natural barriers — must be pushed aside. To all schemes for commercial advancement Carleton lent an ear. The newly appointed Governor of New Mexico, Henry Connelly, one of the most powerful landowners and ranchers in the territory, advocated complete Indian removal. Before the Legislative Assembly, Connelly stated that the "Navajos occupy the finest grazing districts within our limits, and . . . infest a mining region extending two hundred miles north by . . . the same extent east and west . . . [thus] an immense pastoral and mining population is excluded from its occupations and the treasures of mineral wealth that are known to exist . . . have remained untouched. The public interest demands that this condition of things should cease to exist."

And "this condition of things" would cease to exist, if James H. Carleton had anything to do with it. Only two weeks after assuming command of the Department of New Mexico he had laid before the Adjutant General of the Army his preliminary plans for bringing these Indians to their knees. Lieutenant Colonel José Francisco Chavez, Governor Connelly's step-son and second in command to Kit Carson, would soon move into Navajo country with four companies of the recently-raised Fourth New Mexico Mounted Rifles. On the eastern slopes of the Zuñi Mountains, somewhere in the vicinity of Ojo del Gallo, Chavez and his command would establish and garrison a new post. The general location for this proposed fort, to be called Fort Wingate,* had been selected by Canby a year previous, and the choice had been upheld by Carleton as an ideal location from whence troops could "perform such services among the Navajos as will bring them to feel that they have been doing wrong." Seven days after informing the adjutant general of his intentions, Carleton had issued orders selecting the exact site of Fort Wingate. The established military practice of selecting a board of officers to

*Fort Wingate was named in honor of Captain Benjamin Wingate of the 5th U.S. Infantry, who died of wounds received at the Battle of Valverde during the Confederate invasion of New Mexico.

locate a post was adhered to. Representatives of the medical corp, engineers, and the infantry inspected a series of sites. And the one finally chosen was ideal.

Fort Wingate would be located in a broad valley at the headwaters of the Ojo del Gallo, about 85 miles west of the Rio Grande, and four miles south of present-day Grants, New Mexico. The valley spreading out in two directions below the post (one branch leading toward Zuñi, the other to the Pueblos of Acoma and Laguna), afforded fine pasturage. The post would be laid out so that it cut the cardinal points at right angles. A large parade ground would separate officers' quarters from company barracks; and a row of sycamore trees would be planted around the borders of the post, to "assure a cooling shade of a hot summer's day."

Although construction of Fort Wingate begun immediately, erection of actual living quarters was a slow process. A letter from Captain J. C. Shaw, commander of Company A, published in the *Alta California*, revealed actual conditions under which troops lived while the post was being built:

> The fort looks vastly fine on paper, but as yet it has no other existence. The garrison consist of four companies of my regiment — the Fourth New Mexico Mounted Rifles — and we live on, or rather exist, in holes or excavations, made in the earth, over which our cloth tents are pitched. We are supplied also with fire places, chimneys, etc., and on the whole, during the beautiful pleasant weather of the past few weeks, have enjoyed ourselves quite well. Our camp presents more the appearance of a gipsy encampment than anything else I can compare it to.

By spring 1863 the gipsy appearance of Fort Wingate had been rapidly transformed. More than 250,000 feet of lumber had been salvaged from the abandoned Fort Lyon (Fort Fauntleroy); and a contract was awarded to the mercantile firm of Pool and McBride, of Albuquerque, for manufacture of 380,000 adobe bricks for the erection of officers quarters, quartermaster storerooms, hospital, and other buildings. More than a hundred soldiers and civilians were kept working day and night as carpenters, millwrights, masons, and timber cutters. Fort Wingate had to be ready when Carleton gave the word for the army to move against the Navajos.

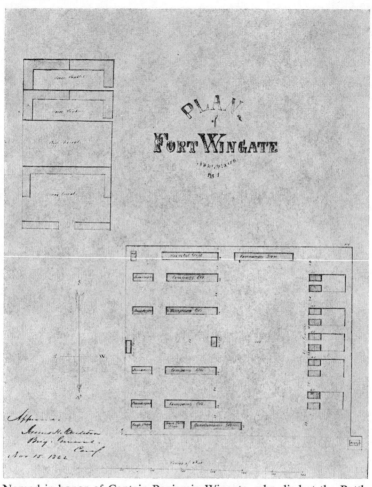

Named in honor of Captain Benjamin Wingate, who died at the Battle of Valverde, this post was the first to be established in Navajo country. From here troops could easily patrol eastern segments of Navajoland, as well as watch the passes of the mountains separating the Indians from the farms and ranches of the Rio Grande Valley.

(Courtesy National Archives)

Chapter Three

A LOG HASTILY placed atop the pile in the corner fireplace gave way, and rolled to the hearth stone with a shower of sparks. In the roomy, whitewashed quarters of the governor's palace, the smell of burning cedar permeated the air, as it did over all of Santa Fe. The snow lay deep, but not so deep as to prevent Navajo headmen from seeking council with the new commander.

Carleton had kept them waiting nearly an entire day, finally ushering the eighteen chiefs into his quarters late in the afternoon; and they sat before him solemnly, wrapped in striped blankets.

Ever since receiving word that the delegation was on its way to Santa Fe, Carleton had mulled in his mind what he would say to the Navajos. His words must be emphatic; not a hint of weakness must creep out — for these Indians were renowned as orators, and gifted at verbal deception.

"I see many familiar faces before me," Carleton began, his interpreter translating a split second behind. "Delgadito, Barboncito, the son of Zarcillos Largos, and others. You honor me by your visit."

Rising to his feet, Dalgadito, the ironsmith and headman from Cañon Bonito, was the first Indian to speak. "General, we see many *blaganas* at Ojo del Gallo; and the *Nakis* come from the east to steal our children and sheep. The Utes, north of the San Juan, paint themselves black and prepare for war. To the south, *blaganas* have chased the Mescaleros and made slaves of many, and I am told that the remainder of the Apaches are in the country of the Comanche.

"Have not the People behaved and complied with the wishes of the white man?" Are the People to be treated as have the Mescaleros?"

Pausing, Delgadito reflected. "We have been beaten. The chiefs before you have suffered defeat. Their women and children are in Mexican families, many are in this pueblo. I myself, have lost two squaws and many horses and sheep, and the stomachs of my people bloat for lack of food."

"This is their game," thought Carleton. "Every time these Indians see a column of troops they come begging for leniency, especially the *ricos*. They with the property, stand the most to loose, and they howl like hungry wolves.

"I know you have all lost children, horses, and sheep, not only in the war which General Canby brought to you, but in past wars as well."

"There are many *ladrones*," declared Barboncito. "They would likewise steal from their own people, if they thought it would further their own end."

"More than a year ago your people promised to hunt down the *ladrones*," accused the commander. "You have not done it — you give only your word to the Army."

"You can have no peace until you give other guarantees than just your word that peace will be kept," Carleton continued unflinchingly. "Go home and tell your people that the Army has no faith in the promises of their chiefs."

By mid-March 1863 Carleton had 400 Apaches interned at Bosque Redondo, where he hoped they could be gradually civilized to a point where they would "become like the Pueblo Indians." Now that the Mescaleros were pacified, troops would be available to campaign against the Navajos. The department commander knew better than to conduct this war against the tribe in the fashion of his predecessors. Previous to the Civil War, the United States Army had conducted a series of abortive campaigns against the Navajos. The use of infantry to chase mounted Indians had accomplished nothing, and all the campaigns had ended with the appearance of the first Navajo delegation voicing a desire for peace.

This tribe was unlike any that Carleton had seen. They were scattered in small family units from the Little Colorado River to the Rio San Juan, and from the San Francisco Peaks to the Rio Puerco of the East — more than 23,000 square miles did the Navajos claim as their domain; and the ruggedness of this country made regular movements of troops impossible. Jugged vermilion mesas; sand that engulfed horse and rider and mired wagons; canyons whose walls rose perpendicular for two thousand feet was what Carleton and his troops faced.

Unlike the Plains Indians, which Carleton had served against, the Navajos never stood and fought. Before soldiers they dispersed, their women and children fleeing to highland sanctuaries, the men playing a game of hide and seek in the labyrinth of redrock cañons, endeavoring to lure the soldiers away from their flocks and families. The strategy to be used against these Indians would be simple and basic — destroy their means of subsistence, hound and harass them during fall; and then deliver a hard, masterly stroke against the tribe when they would feel it the hardest — during dead of winter.

Carleton knew the wariness of these Indians. They would have to be hunted with skill. It would be now that his study of Cossack tactics would be most valuable. In the manner of Russian cavalry, his troops would be kept constantly after the Indians, ". . . not in big bodies, with military noise and smokes, and the gleam of arms by day, and fires, and talks, and comfortable sleep by night, but in small parties moving stealthily to their haunts and lying patiently in wait for them; or by following their tracks day after day with a fixedness of purpose that never gives up. . . ."

Throughout spring troops were withdrawn from Apache country, preparatory to a move on Navajoland. Guides, trailers, and auxiliaries — the eyes and ears of any army — had to be recruited. Carson knew that a campaign against the Navajos would fail unless experienced trackers — who knew the ways and sanctuaries of the Diné — were available. Having been Ute agent for a number of years, Kit was well aware of the animosity which that mountain tribe harbored for their neighbors across the Rio San Juan. War between these people were commonplace, and during times past he had even aided the Ute cause. These Indians would be his first choice as auxiliaries to his troops. "The Utes are very brave, and fine shots, fine trailers, and uncommonly energetic in the field," Carson wrote to Carleton in an effort to sell the general. "The Navajos have entertained a very great dread of them for many years. . . . One hundred Ute Indians would render more service in this war than double their number of troops."

Carson didn't have to pressure Carleton on this point, however. While the old mountain man was harboring thoughts of hiring his Indian friends, the department commander was hard at work organizing companies of irregularies. Volunteers by the hundreds had submitted their names. From Cubero, Cebolleta, Abiquiu, and the Indian Pueblos, units were being formed and equipped at government expense. There would be plenty of caps, powder, and shot for every old percussion rifle in the hands of a Mexican or Pueblo Indian.

Fort Wingate now stood ready. Sturdy outer walls, nearly six hundred feet to a side, enclosed four adobe company quarters and five quarters for the officers. To the southeast, and also enclosed by walls, were corrals for cattle and the mounts of the cavalry. When Carleton personally inspected the post in April, he was more than pleased. The first part of his plan had been completed. From this post troops could advance further into Navajo country to erect still another post, thus cutting the Navajo domain into segments — each segment easily patrolled, and the army thus better able to coordinate its movements.

As soon as grass was high enough to sustain the movement of cavalry, Carleton would send Kit Carson and his regiment to Pueblo Colorado, near present-day Ganado, Arizona, "and there establish a defensible depot for his supplies and hospital; and thence to prosecute a vigorous war upon the men of this tribe until it is considered . . . that they have been effectually punished for their long continued atrocities." At the same time, the garrison at Fort Wingate was strengthened by addition of 315 men, comprising companies E, F, and H, of

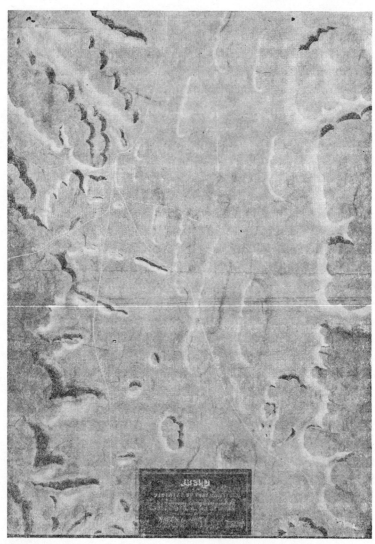

Many historians point to Pueblo Colorado as the location of Fort Canby. Grass and water were in short supply there, and rough terrain made approach to that locality exceedingly difficult. Old Fort Defiance, at Cañon Bonito, was therefore rebuilt and named Fort Canby. This map shows Cañon Bonito as Carson's headquarters. (*Courtesy National Archives*)

the First New Mexico Volunteers. These troops would support and cooperate with Carson's troops; alternating their scouts so that at least two companies would be in the field at all times.

At first glance Pueblo Colorado would be ideal for another military post. It was situated in the very heart of Indian country, and was close to a contemplated cutoff route to the gold fields being developed along the headwaters of the Gila. Careful inspection of the terrain around Pueblo Colorado, however, revealed a total lack of those essentials necessary for maintaining a large military post in isolated country. Water and grass were insufficient for support of cavalry mounts, and the rough terrain rendered approach to the proposed fort exceedingly difficult for wagons. Perhaps Cañon Bonito — the site of old Fort Defiance — would be better as an operational headquarters for Carson's troops.

The burned and ruined skeleton of Fort Defiance, founded by Colonel E. V. Sumner in September 1851, would be rejuvenated. Like everything he planned, the fort which Carleton proposed to erect at Cañon Bonito, would be elaborate. Two story officer and enlisted men's quarters had been drafted by the quartermaster department, and an adobe wall would surround the entire post. Construction on this scale, however, would be held up, for no one was sure how long this Indian war would last. In the meantime, the new post plans would be shelfed, and a temporary sod and log post, slightly larger than the 1851 fort, would serve as Carson's headquarters.

By mid-summer all preparations for the Navajo roundup had been completed and the troops were ready to take the field. As a gallant gesture, General James Carleton sent word to Delgadito and Barboncito — that the war was about to commence. All Navajos not wishing to engage in hostilities would be given until July 20 to come into either Forts Canby or Wingate with their families — and there, await transfer to a new reservation being set aside for them along the Pecos River. After that day, ordered Carleton, "every Navajo that is seen will be considered as hostile and treated accordingly; that after that day the door now open will be closed."

The "door" slammed shut, and Colonel Carson struck the first blow by ordering out small detachments from Fort Canby to harass the Navajos. Throughout the summer of 1863 the First New Mexico Volunteers and their Ute auxiliaries did a thorough job. Thirteen Indians were killed, and more than twenty women and children captured. But what was more important, was that virtually all fields and planting grounds within a forty mile radius of Cañon Bonito, were destroyed. Carson reported that 2,000,000 pounds of Navajo grain had been put to the torch by his troopers.

All springs and water holes known to be frequented by Indians were vigilantly watched by either the army, or by Ute and Pueblo auxiliaries. Patrols from Canby and Wingate scouted the interior of Navajoland, while companies from Forts Bascom, Stanton, Sumner, and from Albuquerque and Los Pinos, were stationed in passes of the mountains forming the Navajo-New Mexico frontier, to intercept Indian raiding parties returning from the Rio Grande Valley. Carleton, fearful that small parties of Navajos might travel southward to join with Gila Apaches, cautioned Brigadier General Joseph R. West to be on the lookout. West was also advised to take steps to meet the increased depredations which were expected as coming snows forced Indians out of the mountain in search of subsistence.

By fall Carleton's scorched-earth policy had taken its toll. With their fields ruthlessly burned and herds driven away or slaughtered — the Navajos faced starvation as sure as the snows would come. On October 21 a Navajo delegation, desiring peace, arrived at Fort Wingate. Unlike other wars with this tribe, there would be no cessation of hostilities upon appearance of the first Indian waving the olive branch. The Navajos were abruptly informed that they had no choice in the matter — "All must come in and go to the Bosque Redondo, or remain in their own country at war." Indians who voluntarily surrendered would be sent to a new reservation — and there, be protected, fed, and clothed. They would furthermore, be permitted to retain all livestock (except those animals bearing government brands). The recalcitrant members of the tribe, however, would feel the arm of the American military as never before.

Although military movements had been carried out with dispatch, and were considered successful, the results of the campaign thus far did not measure up to Carleton's expectations. Only 180 tribesmen had surrendered — indeed a poor showing for a "policy" upon which rested the future economy of New Mexico — if not the very military reputation of its instigator. Instead of giving themselves up, Navajos merely disappeared like magic before the troops; or when out of rifle shot, taunted and jerred the soldiers. Perhaps Navajo reason could be appealed to — and Carleton would try anything which would bring his plans to a successful conclusion. Late in November the general dispatched a delegation of four headmen, lead by Delgadito, to carry word of the comforts which awaited the tribe at Bosque Redondo. The *jornada* of this delegation effected little. Navajos replied by attacking

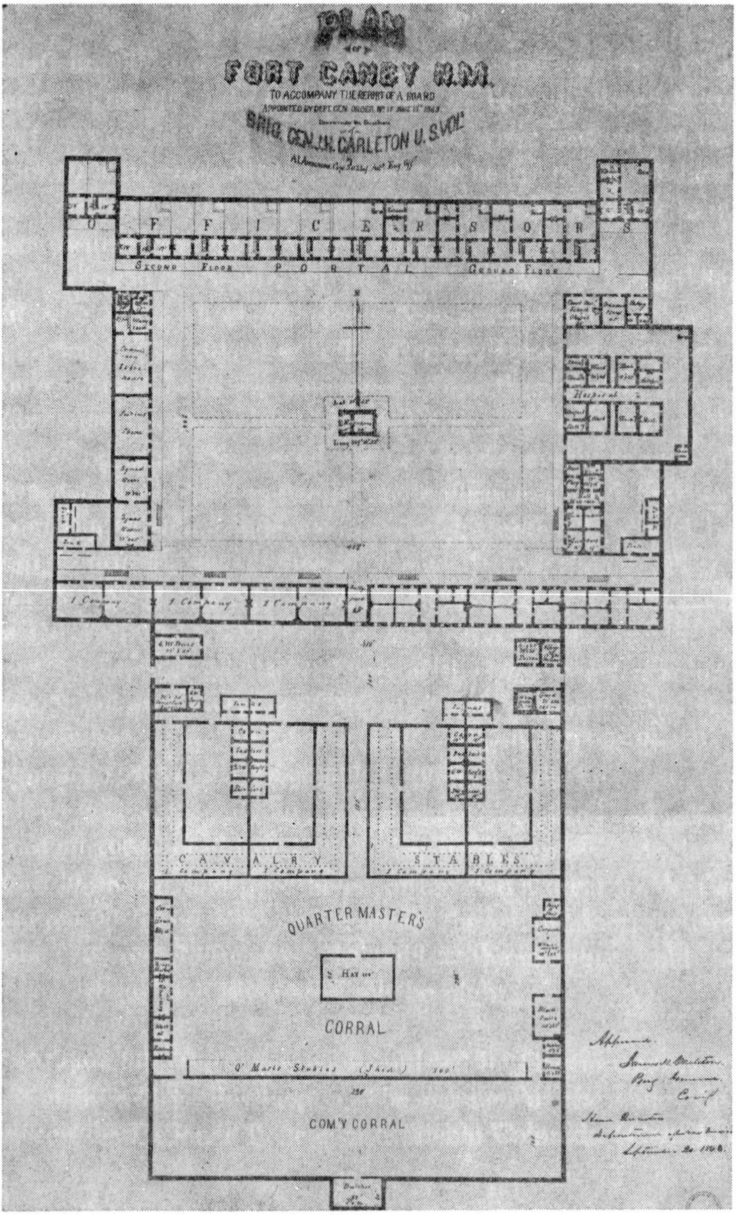
PLAN
of
FORT CANBY N.M.
TO ACCOMPANY THE REPORT OF A BOARD
BRIG. GEN. J.H. CARLETON U.S. VOL.
OFFICERS QUARTERS
SECOND FLOOR
PORTAL
GROUND FLOOR
Hospital
1 Company
CAVALRY STABLES
QUARTER MASTER'S
CORRAL
COM'Y CORRAL

the herds belonging to the Mescaleros at Bosque Redondo; and waylaying a quartermaster train bound for Fort Canby, killing its wagon master, Powell Russell.

With the closing of 1863, however, Navajos had another enemy to contend with. Crops and herds had been drastically reduced by Carson's campaign; and many Indians had been caught by the army before they had a chance to cache subsistence enough to sustain themselves through the ensuing cold months. Now was the time for Carleton and Carson to strike — while the snow fall deeply obliterated forage for the remnants of Navajo stock, and hunger gnawed at Navajo stomachs.

For centuries Cañon de Chelly has been the distinctive landmark of Navajo country. In reality the gigantic cleft is not just a single canyon, but a great drainage system comprising two main troughs, whose vermilion sandstone walls rise perpendicular for nearly a thousand feet, standing in contrast to azure sky and cedar studded rim. Sculptured by wind and water, the main gorge — Cañon de Chelly — winds its way tortuously for thirty miles to head in the gray Chuska-Tunicha Mountains. There it splinters into three tributaries: the Cienega Negra, or present-day Whiskey Creek; the Pala Negra (Palisade Creek); and Cienega Juanica, the Wheatfield Creek of modern maps.

Still another tributary enters Cañon de Chelly from the north-east, four miles above Chinle. Called by the Spanish, Cañon del Trigo, its rock shelters and caves have yielded remains of ancient inhabitants. Archaeologists would, in the far distant future, called it appropriately Cañon del Muerto— Cañon of the Dead.

These cañons had long been thought to be the impregnable stronghold of the Navajos — the general area being vaguely noted on early maps and in Spanish tradition as a "Navajo Fuerte," or Navajo fort. Indeed, there may have been basis for thinking so. The Navajos had long planted the sandy cañon floors to corn and melons; and from the Hopis they had received the first peach trees, which by 1864 had multiplied until hundreds of acres of bottom land were covered with prime orchards — the delight of the Navajos. Along cañon rims Navajos tucked their hogans, hidden carefully from prowling enemies. Sheep, horses, and goats — the status and pride of the tribe — grazed unseen in nearby rincons, close herded by squaws and children.

Because of the tradition that Cañon de Chelly was the sanctuary of Navajos during times of strife, it naturally became a target during military operations against the tribe. Spanish expeditions raided the sinuous cañons throughout the 18th century; and Mexicans, guided by Utes and renegade Navajos, prowled the rim at a later date, searching for slaves and livestock. It was during those troubled years that a number of tribesmen were bottled up in a rock shelter at the upper end of Cañon del Muerto. Ricocheting bullets did a lethal job, and Indian bones lay bleaching for generations; the shelter shunned by all as a place of *Chindi,* or death.

Like their Spanish and Mexican predecessors, Anglo-American leaders directed their movements toward the cañons. Colonel John M. Washington, the first military commander of New Mexico, proceeded to the western mouth of Cañon de Chelly, near Chinle, during the summer of 1849. And the 1851 punitive expedition led by Colonel Edwin Vose Sumner marched directly for the reputed Navajo stronghold.

Again in 1858, Cañon de Chelly was the focal point of a sortie conducted by Colonel Dixon S. Miles.

Although with each expedition knowledge of the chasms increased, it was not until 1859 that an attempt was made to assemble all existing data, and verify it. During summer of that year four separate reconnaissances were conducted by military personnel from Fort Defiance; their chief aim being to pull together all data bearing on the geography of Navajoland. For the first time Cañon de Chelly was thoroughly charted and its features noted for future army movements. When it came time for Carleton and Carson to move upon this target, a great fund of knowledge was at their disposal. In fact, the Rope Thrower, as Kit was known to Navajos, had already profitably utilized the intelligence collected in 1859, which located the larger Indian planting grounds and grazing localities.

Destruction of crops and herds had caused Navajos to move to regions where subsistence could still be procured. Having been spared by Carson, Cañon de Chelly was a haven for Indian refugees. It would be the last point of attack — to be launched during winter, when it would be felt the most. Throughout December 1863 Carson planned his assault. He sifted facts and intelligence for clues as how to approach his objective. Earlier Spanish and Mexican expeditions had penetrated the cañons via numerous side trails, led always by Indian guides. John M. Washington had made a laborious march over the 6,000 foot Defiance plateau, and through the choking red sand beyond, to the Chinle valley and the western mouth of the cañon.

The chronicler for that expedition, Lieutenant James H. Simpson, explored the cañon only to a point beyond White

House ruin. Although the trip was a short one, his practiced eyes were quick to pick up a number of tactical observations: "Should it be necessary to send troops into this canon . . . a force should skirt the heights above to drive off assailants from that quarter, the south bank should be preferred, because [it is] less interrupted by lateral branch cañons." Ten years later another lieutenant, John G. Walker, would again recommend the use of a flanking force on the tablelands above.

Carson's strategy had thus been formulated years before he appeared on the scene. He had only to apply it vigorously and ruthlessly.

On January 6, 1864, two commands filed out of Fort Canby to deliver the blow to the Navajos at Cañon de Chelly. Ex-Ute agent from Abiquiu and now captain, Albert W. Pheiffer, with Company H and thirty-three men of Company E, First Cavalry, New Mexico Volunteers, rode for the east entrance of Cañon del Trigo — Cañon del Muerto of today. The other command — and by far the largest, totaling 400 men — was personally led by the old mountain man, Kit Carson. This latter column would move over the Defiance plateau to the west entrance of the cañons, near Chinle. Between the two units, the Navajos within their "natural fortress" would be bottled up.

Despite the below freezing temperatures, the spirits of the volunteers were high as they moved out from Fort Canby in column of fours. Vengeance perhaps, was foremost in the minds of some New Mexican troops, they having lost property at the hands of Navajo war parties. Others hoped to enrich themselves, for this tribe had always been considered a prime source of plunder. And like all soldiers in every war, the majority prayed that this would be their last Indian scout.

Six inches deep the snow lay, and with each passing mile toward the mountains the white mantle deepened. The march was agonizing, horses and mules slipped and slid on iced rocks. The men, moustaches caked with ice from their labored breathes, hands numb despite gloves and fatigue coats, beat themselves to keep circulation going.

Pheiffer's troops covered only nine miles the first day, and seven the next. For the next three days they labored along the base of the Chuska Mountains, pass Laguna Negra and Laguna Colorado, both frozen solid. The command often divided, as an advance guard of fifteen men, equipped with picks and shovels, broke the frozen trail for the main force, and the rear guard that followed with the supply mules.

The east entrance was finally reached on January 11. Pheiffer knew from long experience the hazards lying within the cañons, and instructed his men carefully before commencing passage the next day. The command would be kept as close together as possible, moving as one body through the cañon. The advance guard would be entrusted to the leadership of Lieutenant Laughlin; the rear of the column, with its precious supply train, would be commanded by Lieutenant C. N. Hubbell. All knew and dreaded what was to come. Roads in the gorge were nonexistent, and the high wall and talus slopes gave cover to snipers, and opportunity for ambushes.

Down the boulder strewn creek bed of what is today Spruce Creek, a tributary of Cañon del Muerto, the command threaded its way. Horses and mules floundered under their heavy loads, and broke through the ice covering of the creek. Troops worked their fingers to keep back frostbite, eyeing the cañon walls nervously. The gorge had not yet begun to climb perpendicular over the heads of the soldiers. Numerous deep rincons came in from all sides, and the talus slopes were overgrown with spruce.

Pheiffer had penetrated the main portion of Cañon del Muerto but a short distance before encountering Navajos. Like mountain cats, the Indians began appearing on rocky ledges high above the volunteers. They threw rocks, cursed the New Mexicans and derided them by exposing their posteriors and threatened vengeance in every variety of Spanish they could muster. They endeavored to detour the troops into side cañons and up rocky paths. It would be tempting to deploy and teach them a lesson, thought Pheiffer. No use though, only a mountain goat or an Indian could make their way through the maze of cañons and rocks.

Again and again the carbines of the New Mexico volunteers spoke. A number of Navajos had underestimated the range of the guns which the soldiers carried. That first day the newly issued Springfields sniffed out the lives of two bucks and one squaw, who "obstinately persisted in hurling rocks and pieces of wood." Six others were captured. As darkness closed in, shutting the cañon up like a great tomb, the command found a secure spot on the cañon floor, "where plenty of wood was to be obtained — the remains of old Indian lodges," and bivouaced for the night.

Meanwhile, the larger command led by Carson was struggling toward its destination. The passage of the valley between the Defiance Plateau and Pueblo Colorado (Ganado) had been slowed. Wind had piled snow drifts several feet high and at times the four hundred men, with their mules and oxen teams, seemed at bay in a white sea. Twenty-seven oxen froze to death on that trip, and one wagon was abandoned, reducing slightly the rations which had been alloted to the soldiers. Although the movements of Pheiffer and Carson had been timed to occur simultaneously, the larger command had arrived at Chinle a day late. In normal weather, Carson could have traveled the distance in one.

On the day that Pheiffer began his passage of Cañon del Muerto, Kit reconnoitered Cañon de Chelly's western entrance, as well as its southern rim, before commencing full scale operations the next day. The near perpendicular walls, falling for a thousand feet or more, convinced Carson of the futility of locating a trail to the bottom of the gorge, whereby he could flank and surprise the Indians.

On the morning of January 13 Carson divided his force. Companies B and G, under leadership of Captain Asa B. Carey, would proceed along the south rim of Cañon de Chelly, while companies C and D, commanded by Captain Joseph Barney, would attempt to march along the northern rim. Carson, growing anxious for word from Pheiffer, decided to accompany Carey in hopes of meeting the lost unit.

For nearly two days Carson and Carey moved cautiously along the south edge of the great chasm, approaching its eastern entrance. Carson found not a trace of Pheiffer. They did verify, however, the earlier conjecture that the south rim of the Navajo citadel could be flanked without much trouble.

On their return to the main camp at Chinle, Carson and Carey were greatly relieved to find Captain Pheiffer and his lost command resting easily. Reason for the two units not meeting now was apparent. The foul weather had shrouded the eastern entrance to Cañon de Chelly, unknowingly Pheiffer had passed it, and had found the entrance to Cañon del Muerto instead, and with that vanished all possibility of a link-up with Carson and Carey.

While the troops rested that night and swapped impressions of their venture through the gorges, three Navajos came into camp under flag of truce. They requested permission to surrender with their families.

"You have until ten a.m. the next morning," replied the Rope Thrower, through an interpreter. "After that time, if you have not appeared, my soldiers will hunt you and your people down." Next morning — well before the designated time — sixty ragged and starving Indians struggled into camp, expressing in Carson's words, "their willingness to emigrate to the Bosque Redondo."

The Indians would have gladly surrendered earlier, had they not thought this war was one of extermination. Owing to Carson's scorched-earth policy, many of their women and children had already perished from exposure and starvation. As this party of Navajos desired to return for the rest of their band, Carson granted them freedom to do so — and directed them to assemble at Fort Canby in ten days.

Wanting to be present when Navajos began arriving at Fort Canby, Kit Carson with the majority of his command, set out on the return journey to Cañon Bonito. He left, however, a unit of seventy-five men under Captains Carey and Pheiffer, to again march through the Cañons, destroying as many hogans, peach orchards, fields, and flocks, as they could find.

Being the senior officer, Carey assumed command of the

detachment left at Cañon de Chelly; and after consultation with Phieffer, decided to travel the south branch of the cañon system — the north having been scouted by Pheiffer. On January 16 the unit moved out. Past White House — the 12th century cliff dwelling — the volunteers moved, noting with interest the yellowish-white rooms perched high above the main ruin. They stopped only to destroy Navajo dwellings and hack down trees.

Throughout that day Indians were seen in the rocks overhead and hovering about the rear of the column as it performed its work of destruction. Occasionally patrols were sent out from the main column, following Indian tracks. Some six miles above the cañon entrance, the New Mexicans struck a trail coming down the south cañon wall. Sheer and precarious, the path — known today as Ladder Trail — showed fresh Indian signs. Through heavy snow the volunteers threaded their way up the trail toward the rim. At the head of the trail, a group of Navajos were encountered. Silhouetted against the snow, they made excellent targets. The first volley killed several, and the rest fled over the mesa top.

At the intersection of Cañon de Chelly and spruce-lined Bat Cañon, Carey and Pheiffer pitched their camp for the night. Late that afternoon Navajos began to come into camp in such large numbers, that by nightfall Carey counted 150 adults, as well as many children. This pitiful group of hungry, cold natives were informed that unless they tendered their "full and complete submission," all would be treated as enemies, hunted down, and destroyed like predatory animals. Permission, however, was granted many Navajos to return for their families — provided, as Carson had stipulated — they would come into Fort Canby in ten days.

With the command's arrival at the east entrance of Cañon de Chelly the next day, its task of laying waste to the Gibraltar of Navajoland had been completed. Carey and Pheiffer then struck a direct line of march for Cañon Bonito, and the warmth and relative comfort of Fort Canby.

The Diné had been hit, and hit hard, by Carson and his troopers. Hogans, orchards, and fields had been laid waste, and flocks too large to drive in had been ruthlessly slaughtered. Inclement weather added to the Indians' miseries. The Navajos were now left but two choices — surrender and be fed by the army, or retreat deeper into the recesses of their land, there to grub out a subsistence on piñon nuts and wild potatoes. Many chose the latter, and migrated with what flocks they could preserve, deeper into the maze of cañons which characterized their homeland. Some pushed northward into the dissected country around Navajo Mountain; others forded the Rio San Juan and sought sanctuary to the north of the river. Still other bands made their way west, beyond the Hopi villages, or to the south, where they joined their cousins, the Gila Apaches. But the majority of Indians, who did not surrender, did what all peoples do when faced with a disaster of this kind. Instead of fleeing into unknown country, they remained close to the redrock land they knew best — ever vigilant against surprise and lurking death which existed in the form of Utes, Puebloans, and the blue-clad New Mexicans.

Chapter Four

By February 1 the more destitute Navajos began to arrive at Forts Canby and Wingate, and by the first week of that month almost 800 Indians were awaiting transfer to Fort Sumner. Thirty days later this number had swelled to 2,500, and still tribesmen poured in, giving the military post the appearance of a Bedouin encampment. "There are at this moment a hundred campfires sparkling amongst the hills of Cañon Bonito and within five hundred yards of this post," an unknown correspondent wrote to the Santa Fe *Gazette*. "These fires are built by peaceful Navajos who have been arriving daily in large numbers. . . . It is a happy omen. . . . There are now about 1600 Indians here, and perhaps an equal number on their way to Fort Wingate, so that at the rate they arrive daily, we will in less than three weeks have about five thousand on the reservation."

This correspondent was not far wrong. In fact, Navajos were pouring into Fort Canby in such numbers that Kit Carson deemed it expedient not to send out scouting parties for fear of hostile encounters with incoming Indians. Throughout the winter months the flow was unabating. By mid-May Carleton and Governor Henry Connelly were convinced that the major portion of the tribe had surrendered, and those Indians remaining in their old country were too few to cause trouble; and a proclamation was issued announcing "a suspension of arms in the prosecution of the war against the Navajo tribe."

The swelling numbers of tribesmen, with their livestock, were cutting heavily into army quartermaster stores. It was imparative, therefore, that the army shift its prisoners from Forts Canby and Wingate to the new reservation, as fast as possible. On February 2, 1864 the first contingent of Indians — some two hundred — were forwarded to Los Pinos on the Rio Grande, where they could be fed cheaply and quickly. A month later, two thousand tribesmen with 473 horses and 3,000 sheep, were shifted from Canby to Fort Sumner. This group was lucky. Blankets were nonexistent at the posts in Navajo country, and the results were inevitable. In little over a week 126 Indians died, many from exposure. Flour had been furnished to tribesmen leaving for Bosque Redondo which was contaminated with rat droppings. Cramps of dysentery struck the Navajos, many crawling to the side of the road, where they perished from exposure. Those Indians unable to resume their march were shot — perhaps mercifully — by their escorts. Of a party of a thousand Indians sent to Fort Sumner, its officer in charge reported ten individuals dying on the road between Cañon Bonito and Los Pinos, the forwarding center on the Rio Grande opposite Albuquerque. There was no mention of the number which perished during the remainder of the journey. Still Navajos continued to surrender, for they had no other choice: surrender, or die a lingering death by exposure and hunger.

Despite the "official cessation" of hostilities against the Navajos, they continued to be harrassed by their traditional enemies. The Utes and Pueblo Indians had no intentions of ceasing their raids, and their slaving and plunder expeditions spurred Navajos to surrender in greater numbers. In mid-April 2,400 men, women, and children were loaded into quartermaster wagons and transported 400 miles to a flat, wind-swept reservation on the open plains east of the Rio Grande. The weather was very inclement. Heavy snows fell, and ensuing gales piled drifts over roads which the Navajos must take. The Indians, many nearly naked, packed into wagons, or forced to walk behind the lumbering vehicles, suffered the agonies of frostbite. Dysentery also took its toll — and the route of their march was marked by the frozen corpses of Indians, who, too fatigued to go on, had crawled to the wayside to die.

Although the Long March or Long Walk — as this episode in Navajo history is known — was an agonizing experience, the real horrors began at the Bosque Redondo reservation. There is no greater shock for a people than to witness the destruction of everything they possess. Homes, crops, and herds — all symbols of prestige and status to these people — were wiped away with one stroke by Carleton's campaign. But the greatest shock of all would be the period of incarceration, and the full effects of that period upon the Indian, his family, culture, and lifeways are beyond the grasp of white man's imagination.

Carleton's predecessor, Colonel Canby, had attained a semblance of peace after prosecuting a vigorous military campaign against the Navajos. This peace, however, was

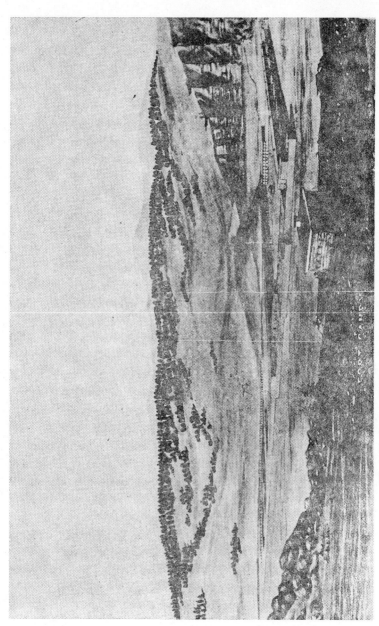

Fort Canby — Christopher Carson's operational headquarters

(Courtesy National Archives)

soon shattered by incroachments on the part of both Indians and New Mexicans. His strategy had ended in failure — like all others for the past two centuries — and only the most stringent measures would alter the situation. There was now little choice between exterminating the Navajos, or removing them to a preserve so removed from the settlements, as to isolate them entirely from the inhabitants of the territory. Canby repeatedly urged the Office of Indian Affairs and his superiors in Washington to undertake such a program. However, James Carleton would be the man to implement this plan.

No sooner had he arrived in New Mexico, than Carleton initiated a program to apply pressure upon Washington for permission to remove the troublesome Indians of the territory. It was by the clamping of martial law upon the territory that Carleton was able to bring his plans to fruitation. Through correspondence with high military echelons, and through influential friends and associates in Washington's political circle, the general pushed the idea of a reservation into proper hands. On January 15, 1864, Secretary of the Interior J. P. Usher, laid before President Lincoln the recommendation for establishment of a forty-square-mile reservation with Fort Sumner as its nucleus. By the following day the Chief Executive had approved the document, and Bosque Redondo was officially recognized as the reservation for the Apaches of New Mexico — without any mention of the tribe which soon would displace the Mescaleros.

By the end of 1863 Fort Sumner was nearly complete. Seven spacious adobe buildings of five rooms each had been constructed as officers' quarters. Six more buildings, each capable of housing 100 enlisted men, were also standing.

There was a hospital of twenty-four beds, a large adobe bake house, as well as a three room guard house. Four storerooms, 175 by 36 feet, sheltered quartermaster and commissary supplies; and three stables, of 100 horses each capacity, afforded protection for garrison mounts.

It is ironic that the first contingent of Navajos sent to Fort Sumner would be the Cebolleta group from the Mount Taylor region. Under the leadership of Sandoval, this partially acculturated band had acted as auxiliaries and guides to Mexican and subsequent Anglo-American punitive expeditions against the major portion of the tribe — their payment being the retention of all captives. In acting as allies to the Mexicans, the Cebolleta Navajos had brought the wrath of their own people upon themselves. Unknowingly, however, General James Carleton had brought retribution when he issued orders that "all must go to Bosque Redondo."

The Cebolleta Navajos, several hundred strong, posed no problem to the more than 400 Mescalero Apaches already interned at Fort Sumner. The surge of captives netted by Carson's campaign, however, quickly altered the picture. Throughout the winter of 1863-64 thousands of Navajos were marched and carted over the trails and roads separating their land from the Llano Estacado.

By mid-March more than 5,000 Indians were encamped for twenty-five miles above and below Fort Sumner. Never in the history of New Mexico had such a large Indian population been assembled in one area — and never before had the essentials for sustaining so many been so lacking. Although Lincoln had given his blessings to the scheme, Carleton had undertaken his "Navajo policy" without having necessary funds and sustenance on hand to support the In-

dians when they arrived. And Carleton's appeals for subsistence and clothing were fanatic. "There are now at and
enroute to Fort Sumner . . . about 5,000 Navajo Indians who
are entirely destitute of everything and it is of *vital importance* that all articles which you have in store such as spades,
hoes, wool cards, shears, ploughs, leather, tin cups and pans,
brass kettles, butcher knives, awls and awl handles, axes,
hatchets, and indigo; also such articles for clothing that is
absolutely necessary for their comfort be sent to them at the
earliest practicable day."

Winter held the Stake Plain in a frozen grip and there was
every indication that the army would soon have thousands of
frozen corpses on its hands unless something could be done
quickly. Sheltering the Navajos was the foremost worry that
beset Carleton. Seeking solution to this problem, the general
consulted his quartermaster officers, who informed him that
large numbers of condemned tents were on hand. When de-
livery date approached, however, the number of tents were
found to be far below that indicated on army supply sheets.
The majority of tents had been cut up and converted to sacks
to transport and store grain, and to meet the needs of an
army in the field. In the meantime, both Navajos and Apaches
were permitted to settle virtually wherever they pleased
within the forty-square miles, and to erect their traditional
hogans and wickiups by whatever means, using materials at
hand.

Throughout that first winter Carleton grappled with ideas
relative to the settling of his prisoners. The native "huts"
were distasteful and aesthetically not pleasing to the general.
He felt the Navajos "must be settled in a pueblo town." By
February 28, 1864, Carleton's "Navajo pueblo" had taken

Sketch of Fort Sumner, 1864

(Courtesy National Archives)

shape in his fertile mind; and he outlined plans for it to the post commander at Fort Sumner:

> The building should be but one story high, and face to the *placitas*. By a proper arrangement — deadwall on the outside, and the buildings arranged so as to mutually defend each other in fighting on the parapets — a very handsome and strong place could be made by the Indians themselves . . . By having a judicious site selected, and the spare time of the families spent in putting up their houses, by next winter they can all be comfortable sheltered. Then to have trees planted to make shade, and I fancy there would be no Indian village in the world to compare it in point of beauty.

For sake of convenience the proposed "Navajo pueblo" would be placed close to the *acequia madre,* the huge irrigation ditch that Apaches and army personel had recently completed. Each Indian family would be given separate plots to farm close by, much like the design of villages and gardens of the Pueblo Indians along the Rio Grande.

To convert Navajos and Apaches into Pueblo Indians is like an alchemist trying to change iron to gold. Both Apaches and Navajos balked at prospects of living in the closed atmosphere of a village community. Accustomed to living in small bands, composed of related members, they instead wished for something reminiscent of what they once had. A series of small villages, each controlled by influential tribesmen was more appealing to them. The tribesmen were accordingly subdivided into nine bands, with the Apaches forming the tenth. Over each division was placed one head chief and six sub-chiefs; these officials being responsible for keeping order and policing their respective divisions.* When assembled,

*The chiefs for the Navajos were Herrero Grande, Delgadito Grande, Ganado Blanco, Delgadito Chiquito, El Barboncito, El Barbon, Narbona,

these headmen would constitute a tribal council for the trial and punishment of all infractions.

As added safeguard, an army overseer was assigned to each band to exercise the will of the United States government. This agent would gather the names of all able-bodied males for labor details. In fact, these overseers could and did control the lives of the Indians — for they had the authority to issue and withhold rations and inflict punishment by any means thought desirable.

In view of the compromise in favor of village band organization, Carleton would have to find a man who knew Indian ways to carry out the tribal reorganization, and no better person could be found than Colonel Christopher Carson. That summer the aging mountain man was recalled from duty in the field and entrusted with supervising the construction of the ten villages. These settlements were no sooner commenced, however, than serious difficulties arose. Navajos, imbued with deep seated fears of the dead, refused to occupy quarters where death had occurred.

Although Carson knew Indian character, he had never before come to grips with the formidable enemies of tradition and superstition. Repeatedly, he tried to reason with the Navajos and convince them they had nothing to fear in a house where death had stalked. To the Diné, however, death and departed spirits were a very real thing, and as expressed by Ganado Blanco, this fear had "grown with their growth and strengthened with their strength." But the army was just as stubborn as the Indians — and Carleton proposed an alternative solution. Adobe dwellings for the Indians would

Judhadore, and Largo. Cadette was chief and principal spokesman of the Mescaleros.

be abandoned, and Navajos would be permitted to retain their tradition "huts." Their hogans, however, would be placed in uniform rows with good intervals and wide streets. One end of each row would be left open for those Indians desiring to move. Then when death struck, a family could immediately destroy their home and move to the end of their row, where a new dwelling would be erected. This solution, like the one previous, proved inadequate. The Navajo had no experience at group living. They had struggled against their environment in extended family units, and they were mistrustful of people outside their own "outfit." The army reluctantly abandoned the idea of settling the Navajos in villages. Instead, the Indians would be allowed to settle in family groups around the confines of the post, close to planting grounds.

True to his word, Carleton was gathering the Navajos together " . . . on a reservation, away from haunts and hills, and hiding places" of their old country. With the bulk of the tribe in captivity, it was now time to begin the formidable task of re-education. It would be tough work to eradicate from Indian minds all "latent longings to commit aggressions." But Carleton felt that new concepts could gradually be passed on to the younger, more receptive Indians, who would eventually replace the old tradition-bound bucks. With a little luck, and a lot of perseverance, a new order would be founded among the Navajos; "the old Indians will die off, and carry with them all latent longings for murdering and robbing, the young ones will take their places without these longings; and thus, little by little, they will become a happy and contented

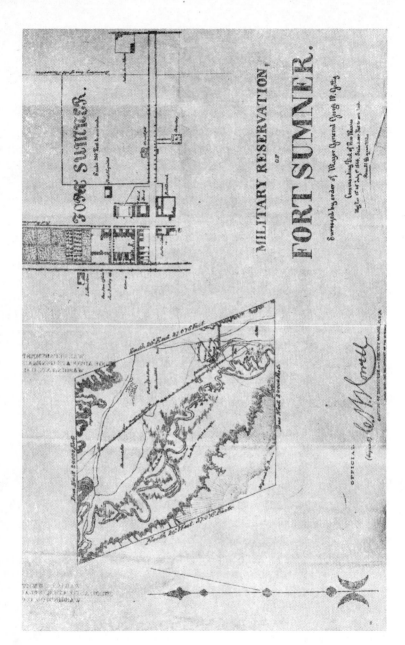

MILITARY RESERVATION,
OF
FORT SUMNER.

people — and Navajo wars will be remembered . . . as a thing of the past."

In April 1863 Carleton took the first step toward re-educating his wards. He requested the Adjutant General of the Army and the Secretary of War to have Fort Sumner made a chaplain post. "If this is done," wrote Carleton, "the Bishop of Santa Fe will send a minister . . . who will teach the Indian children Christianity, and to read and write." At the same time, Carleton was laying his plans before the Right Reverend Lamy, of Santa Fe — and between the two men, a program was mapped to give the Navajos the "rudiments of an education."

By mid-June 1863 the War Department had concurred with Carleton's plan, and Fort Sumner was designated a chaplain post. All that was needed now was a suitable structure for a school, and some "clergymen of energy." Bishop Lamy recommended the Reverend Joseph Fialon as chaplain at Fort Sumner. As this priest was touring Europe and would not be back until August, enough time was allowed the army to erect the school and living quarters. Carleton instructed the commander at Fort Sumner to have Navajos make bricks enough to put up eight "good" rooms for a school and quarters for the priest.

According to Carleton's plans the school would be established near the post. Its rooms would all face a patio or *placita*, where, as the general put it, "the children could play." In overall design, the buildings would be arranged in the same manner as others at the post, facing the same points of compass. Rooms on the north side would be the first erected, the other sides gradually being built until facilities were provided for 800 students.

This first attempt to introduce Navajos to whiteman's education immediately met resistance from the Indians. Navajo children would attend the school so long as their parents thought that additional rations would be forthcoming. When food allotments remained meager the school stood empty. No matter how the army and the Catholic educators approached the teaching of Indian children the outcome was always the same, and by end of 1866 the school was abandoned, and the building converted to quartermaster storage. One observer of Carleton's educational experiment remarked, "I do not think the juvenile savages rightly appreciated the treasure to which it was the key."

The Navajos would respond to the teachings of Christianity and the 3-R's so long as they were being coaxed by the prospects of additional food. Beyond that, the desire for whiteman's education ceased, and his religion became unpalatable. "Christianity," wrote Kluckhohn, "speaks of faroff lands and places which the Navajos cannot visualize; their own stories tell of the four sacred mountains, at least one of which is visible almost everywhere in the Navajo country. The Bible speaks only of a male God and of a society where authority and responsibility centers chiefly in men. Navajos miss Changing Woman, perhaps the principal Navajo divinity, and the whole feeling for the position of women embodied alike in their own social organization and religious lore. The picture of a god who is entirely good is hard for the People to understand, for their whole outlook insists that all beings have an evil as well as a good side."

Carleton's scheme to gradually educate the Navajos, the young replacing the old, was unrealistic. A Navajo, six or seven years of age, is already attuned to his culture. They re-

peatedly have heard the myths and tribal lore, and participated in the small rites of daily life. They have been patients
in curing rites, and have gone with their parents to the
dances, and witnessed the masked impersonators of Navajo
dieties. The imagery, excitement, and fear which these rites
generated were stored in the unconscious long before the
child could reason, or objectify what they saw. By educating
the Navajo according to Christianity principals, Carleton was
only applying a veneer, which cracked the first occasion that
the child re-experienced tribal religious emotion.

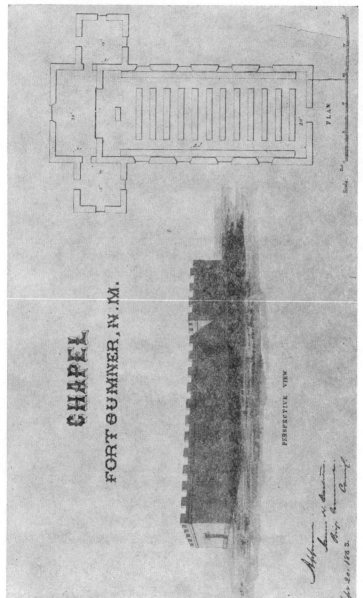

CHAPEL

FORT SUMNER, N.M.

PERSPECTIVE VIEW

PLAN

Chapter Five

As THE Navajo campaign progressed during the early months of 1864, Carleton enlarged his plans relative to Bosque Redondo. He visualized Fort Sumner as a gigantic agricultural experiment station, where the latest farming techniques could be utilized to bring the lands of the forty-square miles reservation into productivity. Certainly upon initial inspection the area had appeared more than promising. The land at Bosque Redondo was flat, with a gradient which allowed easy irrigation from the Pecos; and the topsoil, while sandy, was deep — perfect conditions for growing corn, the staple crop of southwestern Indians.

Navajos were arriving daily, and it was imperative that subsistence be on hand in large enough quantities to feed the tribesmen as they came in. The growing season, however, was well advanced and crops must be planted soon. Feverishly Carleton dispatched letters and orders requesting seeds and tools. By late February two "breaking-up" plows had been procured from Colorado Territory and rushed to Fort Sumner, and two more were being constructed at Fort Union; and would soon be sunk into the earth near the farms commenced by the Mescalero Apaches the year before.

But farrowed earth is unproductive without water, and an irrigation system of immense size and capacity was projected. On February 25 Carleton turned his plans over to Major Henry Wallen, with orders to construct "an *acequia-madre* of great capacity and length, so there will be no doubt of the supply of water being adequate to your needs." To supervise this work, Carleton advised the post commander to select Captain William Calloway, a hard driving officer having considerable experience in both agriculture and engineering.

Under Calloway's direction the acequia, dug by Apaches, was enlarged and lengthened to water an additional 1500 acres lying between the Apache farm and the post. Within a month this tract of land was ready for Navajo occupancy, and thought to be sufficient for the support of the tribesmen then held at Fort Canby.

The arrival, one month later, of 3,000 Navajos quickly altered the situation. Double the acreage would have to be planted if the Indians were to be kept alive. "Every Indian — man, woman, or child — able to dig up the ground for planting, should be kept at work every moment of the day preparing a patch, however small," pleaded Carleton to the post commander. "What with ploughing, spading and hoeing up ground, with the labor of the troops and the Indians, you must endeavor to get at least three thousand acres. It will surprise you to see how much can be done if the bands are properly organized, and all the officers go out and set the example of industry."

Implicitly following Carleton's orders, Calloway commenced a new irrigation system five miles above the post. In less than a month a dam and headgates had been con-

structed; and an *acequia*, twelve feet wide and over six miles
miles long, was laboriously dug. Fifteen miles more of secondary ditches radiating from the *madre* canal were also dug
by Calloway's Navajo laborers.

Once the precious flow of the Pecos had been diverted
onto the parched lands, small tracks of ten to twenty-five
acres were alloted the Indians for cultivation. A great portion
of this land, however, was covered by tangled growths of
mesquite that "had to be grubbed out" before the earth
could be turned with a plow. Calloway set his Navajos to
this task with neither axes nor picks. With their bare hands
the Indians scratched the dirt from the roots, and with stones
and pieces of wood they beat down and broke the tough
roots. This process often compelled an Indian to work all day
on the roots of a single mesquite plant. However, by Navajo
perseverance and industry, Calloway succeeded in clearing
and planting 3,000 acres to corn, beans, melons and pumpkins.

By mid-summer there was every prospect of a bountiful
harvest. The corn alone was expected to yield twenty-five to
thirty bushels per acre — a total of 84,000 bushels. Considering the extraordinary handicaps under which the Indians
worked to reach this goal — scarcity of tools, lateness of
season, militant drivings of army officers — this was an as-
tonishing accomplishment.

When it seemed that the dreams of James Carleton were
at last reaching fruition, fate dealt a lethal blow. The reservation's three thousand acres of prime agricultural land held
every promise of a fine yield. Shortly after the corn had tas-
selled the crop was struck by a cut worm, or "army worm" as

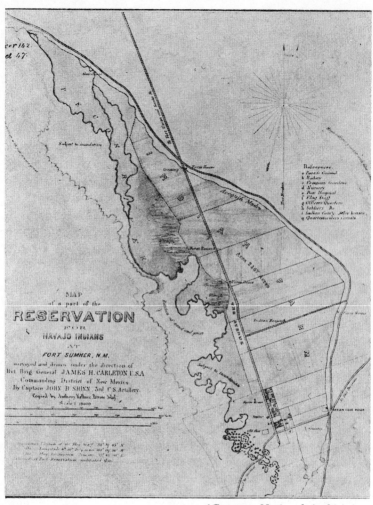

(*Courtesy National Archives*)

it was called, that ate the ears away, unmercifully destroying months of superhuman effort, and threatening to ruin Carleton's policy and bring starvation to the Indians. As though this were not enough, in late October the nearly-matured wheat — which had been planted to augment the corn — was drenched and beaten down by an unprecedented series of cloudbursts. With half that crop gone, Carleton turned to farmers, announcing that army quartermasters would purchase grain and other food stuff in hard currency. But the most productive counties of Taos, Mora, Rio Arriba and San Miguel had not been spared by the storms, as well as by harsh early frosts. While the money was there, the produce was not.

"Fair Carletonia," as Bosque Redondo was being contemptuously labeled by some critics, was nearing the brink of ruin. The reservation was virtually without subsistence, and the numbers of Navajos there was fast approaching the 9,000 mark. The interruption of government wagon trains bringing much needed supplies, by Kiowa and Comanche war parties, heightened an already desperate situation. Indeed, this was the time that would test Carleton's genius for logistics and organization.

On October 22 Carleton took the first step in a series of moves calculated to overcome the plight. "I find that in my judgment it is all-important to reduce the ration of bread-stuffs to twelve ounces per day," explained Carleton to the commandant of Fort Sumner, "and to have issued eight ounces of meat per day . . . until we can hear from the proposals for furnishing wheat, etc. We shall strain every nerve to get a plenty. . . ." In the meantime Carleton instructed the commandant at Fort Sumner to assemble the Navajo and

Apache headmen and present some reason for the reductions of their people's already meager rations.

The Navajos were urged to be "too proud to murmur." The army would strain every nerve to procure enough food. While Carleton foraged the Indians were left virtually to their own resources. Seven thousand sheep, and more than 3,000 horses grazed within the forty-square miles, and this livestock could sustain them for a short time. The slaughter house at Fort Sumner was soon running day and night, butchering the very life and status of the Indians. Nothing was wasted. The head, pluck, and the marrow were issued to the Indians along with instructions on how to make soup "like Frenchmen." In fact, so desperate was the situation that the Navajos had Carleton's implied permission to forage for livestock in Comanche country. In this manner, Carleton would feed his charges and punish his enemies.

By the end of 1864 the Indian population at Bosque Redondo was over 8,000 — a number which taxed Carleton and his quartermasters in their quest for food. It was imperative that no more Indians be sent in. In fact, Fort Canby was being dismantled; and the commanding officers of Fort Wingate, and the forwarding post of Los Pinos, were sent explicit orders to hold all Navajo prisoners where they were until further orders. They too would receive the same rations as their relatives at Fort Sumner.

As the prospects of starvation grew at Bosque Redondo, Navajo resourcefulness came in play. To facilitate easy food allotment at the reservation, a ration ticket system was inaugurated. These would be presented every other day to commissary officers for food quota. It was not long, however, before the army discovered an alarming number of tickets cleverly duplicated. Stamped metal slips were quickly substituted, each with intricate designs which were thought impossible for Indians to copy. Expert in the art of iron working, Navajos were soon producing stamps and dies bearing the marks of the government; and soon 3,000 tickets were counted in excess to the authorized number. Many of these forgeries were so well executed as to be indistinguishable from the genuine article. It was finally necessary to send to Washington for tickets of such intricate design as to be impossible to copy.

In the meantime, the only answer to restlessness was more work as Carleton ordered acequias enlarged, new fields cleared and plowed preparatory to an early planting. At least 9,000 acres — triple the acreage previously planted — would go under the plow in hopes of furnishing all Indian wants, as well as that of the garrison at Fort Sumner. The blight of the "army worm" and the consumption of much of the surviving corn by hungry Indians — who pillaged the fields before the ears filled — convinced Carleton never again to trust in one crop alone. This time at least 3,000 acres would be reserved for wheat which matured early. This land could then be sown to beans during the summer months.

Despite the agricultural failures at Fort Sumner, the post during the early months of 1865, possessed an air of success and industry. A few years before this had been a desolate, uninhabited land, frequented only by Indian raiding parties and itinerant traders from New Mexico settlements. Now a sprawling adobe military post and Indian reservation, with associated fields and irrigation projects, corrals and storehouses stood where there had only been a thicket of cotton-woods.

Every morning army overseers turned the Indians out and marshaled them to the planting grounds on the east side of the Pecos. By the first week of January 6,000 acres had been designated for a variety of crops. Besides the usual corn crop, a large quantity of wheat, pumpkins, squash, musk and water melons, beans, and peas would be sown.

By spring a quadrangle of land embraced by the Pecos River on the west, the *acequia madre* on the north and east, and extending south as far as Fort Sumner, had been planted. More than thirty plows, attended by Navajo labor, had furrowed 5,847 acres. Of this land, 1,000 acres were sown with wheat, which by mid-March had sprouted, and was reporting "growing finely." Three thousand acres more were planted to corn, and the remaining land was devoted to lesser crops.

So promising did the future agricultural yield look, that army personnel began to forget the many trials which during the past year nearly put an end to the Bosque Redondo reservation. Post commandant, Brigadier General Marcellus Crocker, was among the optimistic. If all went well during the planting season, and a full 6,000 acres could be harvested, he believed that the congressional appropriation for food could be abolished altogether. Playing safe, he calculated upon a rather low average acre-yield of 1,500 pounds of grain, which at 6,000 acres gave an estimated nine million pounds. This amount, Crocker figured, would give every Indian "a fraction less than three pounds . . . per day for 365 days." Added to the yield of the farms, Crocker hoped that produce from the gardens would add enough "to subsist the

Indians now at Bosque Redondo, as well as any others that may come in."

By early summer 1865 this crop was almost ready for harvest — and appeared to be unblighted by disease or insect. Upon closer inspection, however, it was discovered that tiny larva were beginning to hatch from eggs laid in the moist silk of the growing ears. The silken strands leading to the points where kernals would develop had again been impregnated with eggs of the "army worm." The embryo kernels of corn were stunted in their growth. The disaster of the year previous was being repeated, and no increase in acreage of farm land would forestall it.

When the final harvest had been completed and the produce weighed and tallied, the results were heartbreakingly below expectations. The corn totaled 423,582 pounds; the wheat planted to sustain the Indians through just such an emergency as this, amounted to only 34,113 pounds. For lesser crops, only 30,403 pounds of pumpkins, and 3,500 pounds of beans were harvested. All this fell far short of the estimated nine million pounds of foodstuffs from the 6,000 acres. Again the Indians would be fed from army commissary supplies — supplies of such poor quality that they had been rejected by government inspectors as army fare, and transferred to Fort Sumner as food for Indians.

Two years of crop failures took the wind out of Carleton. With Congress appropriating funds to feed his charges at Bosque Redondo, there was no need for the general to plead with his post commandant and quartermasters for the conservation of resources. In fact, the army had just about washed its hands with trying to grow anything at the reservation. They were more than happy to turn the responsibility of

Navajo agricultural work party with army overseers

(Courtesy National Archives)

supervising the agriculture at Fort Sumner over to anyone who volunteered for the job. And the new Navajo Indian Agent, Colonel Theodore H. Dodd, arrived on the job in time.

Years of bickering between the army and the Office of Indian Affairs had prevented the appointment of a resident agent for the Navajo Indians. However, the years of 1865-66 marked a cooling of the conflict between the two jurisdictions, and with Colonel Dodd being an ex-army officer and veteran of the Civil War in the west, as well as a member of the board of officers convened to select the site of Fort Sumner, he was very acceptable to General Carleton. Knowing that all previous crops had failed at Bosque Redondo, Dodd urged as early a planting as possible — to avoid "plant destruction by insects." He also knew of the great difficulties with which the Indians worked, and he was sympathetic. No one could plant decent crops without adequate tools, and he requested immediate approval from the Department of the Interior to purchase a large quantity of first-rate agricultural implements, including twenty-five breaking-up plows, a threshing machine and a reaper, as well as hundreds of shovels and spades.

Obtaining congressional approval for purchase of these items, Agent Dodd proceeded to St. Louis, where he bartered for these much needed supplies. After assembling the implements, as well as clothing for his destitute charges, Dodd procured fifty yoke of cattle to haul the supplies to New Mexico. Reaching his destination, Agent Theodore Dodd moved into the adobe quarters formerly used by Lorenzo Labadie, the Apache agent. However, the wretched two rooms constituting the agency, soon proved inadequate for both administrative and storage needs. But Dodd detailed Navajos to repair the old structure, and soon a new room, 20 by 60 feet, was added. With wood hauled from the Capitan Mountains — a distance of 100 miles — a sixty square foot corral was also erected, as well as a fence enclosing ten acres adjoining the agency.

Regardless of the new agent's boundless energy, tragedy struck the Navajos a third time. The 1866 crops failed miserably. The 2,500 depleted, alkali impregnated acres of the government farm, which was maintained solely by the army, produced little over 3,000 bushels of corn — and the bulk of Indian food would have to come from army subsistence stores, which would amount to $582,513 for a nine month period. Failure of the army supervised government farm convinced Dodd that other measures would have to be pursued, if a crop was going to be raised at all. He advocated reducing acreage of the military controlled farm to a mere 1,500 to 2,000 acres, and letting Navajos farm the remaining land by their age-old, tried and proven techniques of planting. "Give an Indian a piece of land as his own," believed Dodd, "and implements to work with, and seeds to plant, and he will go to work with a will, and raise good crops."

By now, however, Navajos had little incentive to cultivate the soil at Bosque Redondo. They had experienced one failure after another. The brackish water they drank brought dysentery; and the garrison infected them with syphilis and gonorrhea. Balking at the twelve hour day labor, Navajos had to be forced to work at bayonet point throughout the early months of 1867.

During March Dodd also had a good many Indians at work constructing a new *acequia,* which commenced near the issue house and ran along the Pecos, parallel to the adjacent hills. By April 1 this ditch was complete and ran for three miles, enabling Navajos to cultivate several hundred acres more. However, the efforts of Dodd and his Navajos were wasted — that year would, like the rest, prove disastrous. The Pecos River shriveled to a mere trickle, and planting grounds parched and cracked under intense summer sun. Whatever crops survived were destroyed before harvest time by severe hail storms.

Three consecutive years of crop failures had destroyed every vestige of desire on the part of the Indians to cooperate with the army. Only uncertainty filled Navajo minds — uncertainty about whether or not the army was able, despite all the promises, to feed them. Even when the Indians practiced their own planting techniques, which had nearly always been productive, the results were the same. Nothing would grow at Bosque Redondo.

Regardless of army promises of protection to Navajo herds, Indian livestock had been ruthlessly garnished. Only 1,550 horses, 20 mules, 950 sheep, and 1,025 goats remained. This pastoral people, who once were credited with possessing a quarter million sheep and sixty thousand horses, had lost everything. The Navajos had been taken from their sacred lands — where everything remained in a state of equilibrium — and had been placed at Bosque Redondo where only disaster struck. They once had fine corn fields and peach orchards, and sheep and horses — wealth and prestige. They now had nothing. Their whole world had been turned up-side-down.

Navajo camp site at Fort Sumner

(*Courtesy National Archives*)

Chapter Six

EVER SINCE arriving in New Mexico Carleton had hoped that his military movements could be expanded to net the territory's entire Apachean-speaking population. Certainly he had not overlooked any detail pertaining to the reservation which would be the Indians' final destination, and hopefully, their permanent home. Long before the Indians had arrived, their camps had been planned. Fields, gardens, irrigation systems, storehouses — everything that was necessary to sustain a large population — came from the fertile mind of the general, was passed to his engineers and quartermasters, and then into reality by Indian labor.

To any military commander, the prime consideration to placement of a military post was control of factors affecting the health of the garrison. Carleton had not only a large contingent of troops to think about, but a sizeable Indian population as well — perhaps the largest Indian population ever assembled in the United States up to that time. The team of officers that had inspected Bosque Redondo were not at all confident of the healthfulness of the location, and were reluctant to recommend the area as site for Fort Sumner. In his refusal to listen to the opinions of these officers,

Carleton courted disaster. He had handled logistics and quartermaster problems long enough to judge the desirability of any area. The other details attendant to the establishment of a military installation such as sanitations, liquor control, and general hygiene he could also control in usual military fashion. The hygienic welfare of the Indians, while approached from the standpoint of an army manual, also bore Carleton's personal touch.

The hospital, which would serve both the garrison and the Indians, was one of the first structures commenced at Fort Sumner. Because Carleton personally inspected — if not planned — every building in those early months, it too was as much a part of him as if he had laid its cornerstone. Built of adobe brick, the building was 170 feet long and 25 feet wide, with wings running back from each end; and the whole compound was enclosed by a wall. Its thirty-inch walls made the quarters quite cool during the summer and retained warmth during the winter months. In nearly every aspect this hospital was of the best design and construction, and in all probability was one of the finest medical wards in the Southwest.

Dr. George Guyther, who had been the physician at Fort Wingate, as well as a close confidant to Carleton, was put in charge of medical affairs at Fort Sumner. And the staff of orderlies and assistants was well-trained in view of current medical practice. Guyther, like his commander, was particularly impressed with Bosque Redondo and had overruled the critical evaluation of the board of officers that inspected the area. Guyther considered Bosque Redondo one of "the healthiest places" he had ever lived in. The doctor reported the site was "peculiarly healthy because of its locality upon an open plain, its freedom from stagnant waters, the ability to prevent liquor at the post, and the power to enforce hygienic laws, are the forces which combine to produce the healthy condition. . . ."

During the first year of Guyther's residence at Fort Sumner, the Indian traffic through the hospital was relatively light, and certainly substantiated the doctor's beliefs. The average number of in-patients seldom were more than twenty-five, and the number of outpatients hovered around seventy. No more than two deaths per month were reported by medical authorities, although there must have been more. Beginning in late 1864, however, the medical day books — records bearing the handwriting of Guyther — began to reveal a far different story.

Three hundred cases were admitted to the hospital during September of that year; and the following month the doctor and his staff administered to two hundred Indians, of which six died of advanced syphilis. During the remaining months of 1864 and into January of the following year, an epidemic of mumps ravaged the reservation. Despite Guyther's claim to the absence of stagnant water about the Fort Sumner preserve, early summer brought a dwindling of the Pecos, and the brackish water standing in the river channel became a haven to mesquitoes. Malaria now became a common entry in the day-books for both garrison and the Indian population at Fort Sumner.

The most troublesome ailments at the post, however, were those of venereal origin. While both gonorrhea and syphilis were rampant, the latter was the most difficult to control. Guyther, however, reported that this disease "were of long standing, little of it . . . being the result of recent communication." Whether or not the syphilis was of recent origin or not, what with nearly 9,000 Navajos living in close proximity to one another, the result was inevitable. At times there were as many as eighty Indians being treated simultaneously for the disease — many of them showing the rash and chancre of primary infection.

The "pure and abundant" water at the reservation soon was discovered to produce not only malaria-bearing mesquitoes, but a "temporary relaxation of the bowels," which in most cases Guyther explained "greatly benefited the persons." Regardless of what medical personnel reported, the Navajos nevertheless suffered; and the soaring sick and death rate at Bosque Redondo would soon become one of Carleton's greatest worries. He had seen what whitemen's disease had done to the Plain's Indians; and there was every chance that illness would cut deeply into the efficiency of the garrison. It was imperative that the troops at Fort Sumner be maintained in top shape, for they virtually controlled the peace of the territory. Whether or not venereal disease was being transmitted from Indian to soldier, or visa versa, mattered not at all. Isolation for the Indians would be the answer.

Stringent orders were issued restricting fraternization between troops and Indians; and on July 4, 1865 orders were issued separating the Indian patients from those of the garrison. The army would continue to use the spacious hospital at the post, but the Indians would be treated in a building near the village of the Cebolleta Navajos. Only nine small rooms, none larger than 15 by 16 feet, were allowed for administering to more than 9,000 Indians. From that date onward, the army saw a drastic decline in the number of Navajo and Apache patients. But sickness and death nevertheless struck.

"Scarce an Indian comes near their hospital," wrote Guyther. "On some days none at all; yet sickness is plentiful among them. The rattle and song of the medicine men may be heard in many huts. The blackened bodies, close cut hair, destroyed huts — the common signs of sickness and death — are very frequent sights. But the daily report of the steward is: 'No one comes here now, doctor.'"

Army officers could not fathom why the Indians avoided treatment when they so desperately needed it. But today the reasons are very apparent. Although Navajos distinguish between contagious infections and generalized psychosomatic illness, all ailments, be they mental or physical, are considered to be of supernatural origin. Physiological causes of disease is completely foreign to Navajo beliefs. Continual misfortune like destruction of property, bodily injury, as well as disease, stem from violations of Navajo religious practices, contacts with ghosts, or witch activities. The treatment of such ailments, therefore, must be directed toward causive factors and not toward the disease. The supernatural beings had to be appeased, and all supernatural relationships restored to normal.

In a hospital, isolated from his family and relatives, forced to live by a strange routine and partake of unfamiliar food, a Navajo is lonely and homesick. Illness is everywhere, and he feels utterly unprotected, disliked, and venerable to all that is evil. The medical practices of the white man bewilders the Navajo patient. The Anglo-American doctor appears to the sick Indian as a totally unrational person. The medic comes only once a day — and for a short time at that. Amid

Navajo corn husking party at Bosque Redondo, 1865

(Courtesy National Archives)

questions, he administers a little medicine, takes the temperature; the rest of the time the Indian must lay still, hour after hour. But the Navajo medicine man indulges the sick; he is there all the time, with lots of medicine; and he treats every portion of the body.

Faced with a soaring disease rate, the causes of which they could not understand, Navajos turned from the military doctors and sought their medicine men, who gave them what they desired most: "of being succored and loved." As Captain Bristol wrote on August 23, 1865, "they say they have more faith in their medicine men than in our doctors; that both effect cures, while death occurs with both; they [nevertheless] prefer to take the chance among their people."

The army, not understanding the reasons behind Navajo withdrawal, sought a scapegoat in the native medicine men; and Doctor George Guyther was the first to launch the attack:

> Thus sickness has begot fear, fear begot superstition, and this nourished fear; they are sick, they die, and the frightened survivors lend an easy ear to the croakings of their medicine men, who warns them that he alone can throw out the demon who, as he says, afflicts them.
>
> Credulous and fearful they obey the order to refuse our medical help and willingly yield entire obedience to these imposters, who though seldom failing to rob them, as fees, of every portion of their property; generally by the passive character of their treatment, consisting mostly of singing, shaking of rattles, and on arrangement on the ground of magic stones, bird claws, antelope hoofs, etc., manage to let the invalid die. The power of these imposters is much on the increase . . . It is not also desirable that the political influence of that fraternity (the native medicine men) ac-

quired by their profession, and more likely to be used in-juriously than beneficially, should be weakened.

A tirade against Indian practioners affected nothing. In fact, it may have been utterly without foundation. The In-dians were merely carrying out the ritual patterns estab-lished by their culture. True, the medicine man was an expensive luxury, nevertheless, he was indispensable to the Indian. The value which Navajos derived from ceremonials were literally bought and paid for. Then as now, a fee is always paid to the singers — otherwise their curing rites are not effective. All ceremonials among these people are costly, and some very expensive indeed. When struck by illness, poor and only moderate prosperous families stand a very good chance of being rendered bankrupt by having to provide a long succession of ceremonials for ailing family members. The army's fear of medicine men came not so much from the latter's ability to bleed the families of their patients, as it did from the fear that the rites would call into action a social organization which was thought to be potentially dangerous. To carry out the divinations the help of many persons were needed: to gather the plants and materials, to carry on subsidiary activities of preparing food, maintain-ing fires and providing water; and to pay the singer and his associates. It was this reciprocity which the army viewed with alarm, and mistakenly considered as a marshalling of strength against the military system.

But this social organization centered around the patient and the practioner, and was not of a hostile nature — it was not bent on overthrow of the army. Its only function was to release pain and suffering: to restore order to the Navajo world. On their own ground — back in their old country —

tribesmen could express their hostility in a brutally harsh manner — behavior that the military could understand and cope with. But in a situation which was controlled by white men, and where disease was rampant — as at Bosque Redondo — Navajos manifested their discomfort and resistence passively. They withdrew from the source of irritation and pain.

Faced with this withdrawal, which affected every aspect of the Bosque Redondo experiment — from governing of the reservation to agriculture — Carleton took steps to put the Indians back in line. He utilized the Cebolleta Navajos, the first group to be settled on the reservation, as a pilot group. To him and every other officer they were Navajos — the only difference was that these Indians had lived in proximity to whites long enough to adopted a few "civilized" traits. He had used this band to construct adobe dwellings in hopes that the rest of their tribesmen would follow suit. Now he moved the Indian hospital to land adjacent to the Cebolleta Navajos.

Much to Carleton chirgrin this move produced bewildering effects. Conflict between the two peoples flared immediately, and the Indians sullenly avoided their hospital even more than before. To the majority of Navajos, the Cebolleta band was just as alien as if they had been Pawnee or Mexican — in fact, perhaps even more so, for to this day they are called among their own people, *Diné'anaih*, or Enemy Navajos. And enemies they were in a very real sense. They had a long history of serving the Spanish, Mexicans, and later, the Anglo-Americans. During the 1840s and 1850s they practiced, under their leader Sandoval, a lucrative slave trade, stealing women and children from their fellow tribesmen, and trading them as menials in towns up and down the Rio Grande. Resentment against the Cebolleta Navajos ran high, often being released in rumors and intimidations that witches, ghosts, and evil beings of all sorts, resided near Cañoncito and Cebolleta — the former residence of the Cebolleta group. They bore the stigma of witches. Little wonder the majority of the Navajos at Bosque Redondo wanted no part of this group, or any program that they were involved in.

The situation at Bosque Redondo — complete Anglo control, failure of crops, disease, and death — resulted in bewilderment, frustration, and aggression on the part of tribesmen. The Navajo's innate fear of illness and death was heightened; and when all remedies failed, and death increased in Indian camps, only one cause could it be laid to — the machinations of evil shadowy personages of the world of the dead — witches and ghosts.

How rampant witchcraft tales, and their associated manifestations were, will never be fully known. The fact that belief in witchcraft was present, however, is attested to by Captain H. B. Bristol:

Witchcraft is practiced among them to an alarming extent. The interpreter informing me that he has seen an Indian apparently in perfect health drop dead. The witches at one time put the evil spirit in his wife; she was about to die, when some . . . (medicine man) administered a little bear's gall . . . and she immediately recovered. It is believed that a witch can pierce the heart of one of her enemies at almost any distance with the quill of a porcupine, or that she can extract one in some manner from between or through the ribs so as to not affect or hurt the person . . . Their ceremonies and manoeuvres . . . are done in secret and by a select few.

In his classic study, *Navajo Witchcraft,* Clyde Kluckhohn points out that witchcraft beliefs, rather than practices, serve not only a dramatic value (a good story) in Navajo society, but offer solutions to problems that are perplexing, and thus disturbing to emotions. Stubborn illness that does not respond to traditional curing rites, and death without visible cause, can be attributed to the machinations of witches.

In a very real sense, witches are scapegoats, and have played a role in all social structures since Paleolithic times. European beliefs in witches are quite obtrusive. They may be a minority within the society, as in the case of the Jews in Nazi Germany; or they may be an external society, as with the Communists versus the Fascists. As modern-day Anglo-Americans have their left-wingers and right-wingers, the Navajos have their witches. And here lies the answer to the Navajo avoidance of the hospital at Bosque Redondo. In all probability the structure's location near the camp of Enemy Navajos, and its connection with death and illness, made it synonymous with witchcraft.

The avoidance of the army hospital, osterization of the Cebolleta Navajos by fellow tribesmen, and the spread of witchcraft tales were indications that the tribe was taking steps to free themselves of a situation that was extremely repugnate to them. Aggressions arising from stressful circumstances — threats to life and health, discomfort from malnutrition, pain, cold fatigue, and disease, combined with fear and bewilderment on the part of tribal leaders could only be endured but a short time. An escape valve had

The Indian commissary at Fort Sumner

(Courtesy National Archives)

to be found — and witchcraft, pathelogical rumors, and the finding of scapegoats were the answers.

The guiding principle behind all army movements in the Far West was the assumption that the military was but an extension of the economic destiny of the white man. Since the Indian stood in the way of exploitation of western regions, he had to be removed — forcibly if necessary. And the inevitable relocation was always carried out with little regard to maintaining past traditions and social values of the Indian. The one basic principle which Carleton could not see, or refused to see, was that groups of people cannot carry out actions for which they have no established social organization. To force a group to take on traits for which no established patterns existed was to invite disaster.

Although the Bosque Redondo experiment gave an impression of order and consistency — that the Navajos were a socially integrated and functioning community — the most prominent condition was one of disarticulation and the absence of accustomed habits of human relationships. Family units had been disrupted by Carson's roundup, and at this reservation Navajos were strangers to each other in a strange situation. What with family ties broken, it naturally followed that traditional political mechanisms would likewise vanish — that was precisely what Carleton had planned.

The Navajos at Bosque Redondo had no precedent for the regimented political system which the military imposed upon them. In pre-Bosque Redondo days there was a semblance of an all-encompassing political system — the *natchit,* or all-tribal assembly. Periodically this group met to discuss internal problems, and consisted of twelve speakers of peace and war. Although today there is debate as to the effectiveness of this organization, its last meeting was nevertheless held shortly before commencement of the Bosque Redondo period, in 1861 to be exact.

The concentration camp atmosphere at Fort Sumner forever did away with this traditional Navajo political organization, although some writers believe that the army village system, as designed by Carleton and Carson, was an attempt to simulate the *natchit*. The regimentation of Navajo life at Fort Sumner, however, did produce a set of petty leaders, who pantered to the whims of the military, as well as a contrasting group of Navajos who developed considerable status among their people for their ability to out-smart the army by either avoiding capture in their old country — as in the case of Manuelito — or who were particularly profficient at pilfering livestock from government herds, and produce from the Mescalero and army gardens. These two groups could well be likened to the *pobres* or *ladrones* versus the *ricos* of the pre-Bosque Redondo days. As in early years, the conflict between these two groups became readily apparent, reaching a crisis stage by late 1865.

Depredations upon government herds were the natural consequence of food shortage. The fact that many Navajo chieftians supported the army against Indians who would raid military gardens, often tracking the culprits down, brought on the wrath of their own people. Lesser chiefs such as Largo, Narbona, Delgadito Chiquito, and the son of Sandoval, of the Cebolleta Navajos, aided the military commander more than other Indian leaders. It is not at all surprising to find army medical records reflecting a higher rate of violent deaths among members of these bands, than for members from groups who allegiance were to such chiefs as Ganado Blanco, Herrero, and Delgadito — men who not only preserved the love and admiration of their people during the Bosque Redondo period, but long after their release from captivity as well. Sparsity of military citation and the traditional Navajo avoidance of death unfortunately often leaves the researcher in the dark for background causes of these deaths. But suspicion and pathological venting of aggression — all reasons for homicide — must certainly have been present at Bosque Redondo, even to a larger degree than what exists today among the Navajo.

The Bosque Redondo Reservation had been initially set aside for the Mescaleros, and whatever other Apaches that could be snared by the army. Upon the border of the Llano Estacado, on their traditional land, these people would be slowly civilized — so it was hoped — by introducing them to agriculture, education, and Christianity, as well as a semblance of "organization and government."

Carleton's campaign was swift and effective. Using every available unit, as well as the Mescalero's natural enemies, the army closed in upon the tribe with a pincer movement. By fall of 1863 the Mescalero campaign had ended, and 425 members of that tribe were residing at Fort Sumner.

Carleton first fed and clothed the destitute tribesmen — and then began his program to re-educate them. Tribesmen possessing outstanding qualities of leadership and who were apparently respected by their people, were sought by the army as tribal leaders. Cadete and Ojo Blanco were chosen as head chiefs, and entrusted with the responsibility of keeping order and drawing rations for their people.

To the commandant of New Mexico the Mescaleros appeared as a challenge. Unlike the Navajos they were not pastoral, nor were they cultivators of the soil. They were raiders, who for generations had raised hell throughout the Southwest and deep into Mexico as well. Break their desire for the plunder trail and make them farmers upon a reservation was indeed a large order.

Carleton perceived the similarity in language between the Navajos and the Mescalero Apaches, and hoped that their differences were due primarily to environment. And for the first six months of their incarceration at Fort Sumner, the Mescaleros almost proved Carleton's assumption that they too possessed traits of agraianism. Aided by Mexican labor, these Indians constructed an irrigation system nearly two miles in length, three feet deep and four feet wide, and planted to grain several large plots of ground. The general, however, had deluded himself. The old adage, "that there was never a hoe made that would fit the hand of an Indian," was never more true — when it came to the Mescalero Apaches.

In reality they were a Plains people and possessed traits derived from centuries of close contact with other peoples dwelling throughout that geographical area. Their culture was oriented to the chase and the raid. Although they were Apachean in speech and genetic makeup, the Mescalero's economic ties were with the Comanche, Kiowa, and other south Plains peoples. They were not sowers of seed by any stretch of the imagination. Out of more than 400 Mescaleros at Bosque Redondo, only eight-six submitted to the disgrace of tilling soil.

Every attempt the army made to settle these people in closely supervised villages met with utter failure. Their nomadic life was indelibly stamped upon them. Suspicious of aliens, always on the lookout for raiders from outside the reservation, they lived like they did upon the plunder trail: moving camp often, never remaining in any one place for more than a week or ten days. To the more perceptive observers of the workings of the new social order at Bosque Redondo, these would have all been signs that the Mescalero experiment was doomed to failure even before the first Navajos appeared.

With the arrival of Navajos at Bosque Redondo in late 1863, the problems of the Mescaleros were only compounded. The sudden tide of Navajo prisoners engulfed the Apaches. Much of the latter's fields were alloted the newcomers, and it was not long before the Fort Sumner reservation was monopolized by a people whom the Mescaleros could never trust, and whom during times past, had considered enemies. Now a minority, surrounded by distasteful cousins, the Apaches manifested every desire for a separate reservation. All the army would grant, however, was permission for them to move about the forty-square mile reserve, establishing their camps wherever they pleased — and this the army granted only in an effort to forstall difficulties between the two tribes.

By late spring 1864 the Apaches were outnumbered by the Navajos four-to-one, and the feeling of anxiety between the two peoples increased to a point where there was speculation as to how long a semblance of peace would last. The crisis finally arrived when Navajos killed a number of Apache horses, which resulted in like retaliation; and Apache tensions were heightened still further by a number of "teswin" making sprees. On the night of April 25, Ojo Blanco slipped away from the reservation with forty-two of his followers. In months to come conditions between the Navajos and the remaining Mescaleros became intolerable.

Besides vastly outnumbering the Apaches, Navajos were endowed with a capacity for not forgetting past grievances between the two tribes, and it was not long until the Apaches became the scapegoat of Navajo aggression, engendered by the disruption of their social and value system. Apache gardens and livestock were raided by hungry Navajos, and squabbling went on incessantly between the two peoples. Only a garrison of 400 soldiers prevented bloodshed. This potentially explosive situation finally reached a climax on the night of November 3, 1865. Under cloak of darkness 335 Apaches, after helping themselves to more than 200 Navajo horses, deserted the reservation and headed southward. Only nine enfeebled and aged members of the tribe were left behind.

The stereotyping of the Indian — which was characteristic of mid-19th century military outlook — had brought disaster to Bosque Redondo. When Carleton moved the Navajos in with the Mescaleros he violated one basic principal — that "there are profound differences in beliefs, sentiments, habits, and customs among peoples, tribes, and communities." That these differences were never preceived and understood by army administrators, from the department commander down to post commander, was brought forcibly home the night the Mescaleros left the reservation.

The mass decampment of the Mescaleros did not end the conflicts between Navajos and other Indian groups however. One of Carleton's foremost reasons for locating Fort Sumner in the Pecos Valley was to erect a barrier to Comanche and Kiowa incursions, both westward into New Mexico Territory and southwest into Mexico. In fact, he could not have picked a better spot for situating a military garrison. The cottonwoods at Bosque Redondo had for generations been the terminal point for homeward-bound raiding parties. From there trails radiated in every cardinal direction. Trails from the east converged upon this rendezvous to link with western paths bringing trade with the Gila Apaches; or south to Mexico where lay the rich ranchos and mining regions of Chihuahua, Durango, and Sonora; or north to the trading towns on the upper Pecos and Rio Grande.

If there was any group of people which could be labeled as traditional enemies of the Navajos, it would be those "Lords of the south Plains." Without exception, every account of Navajo-Comanche contact was of a hostile nature — and now Carleton had established these mortal enemies as neighbors.

Compared with Texas and the northern states of Mexico, the Territory of New Mexico had few problems with the Comanches. For decades an unrestrained commerce had existed between these Indians and the Mexican population. Thousands of head of cattle stolen from Texas ranchos, as well as from Mexico, were driven into the territory where a ready market awaited them. Unknowingly Carleton — as well as previous department commanders — had contributed to this trade. The few licenses he had issued to New Mexicans to trade with Comanches were being passed from

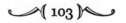

Indians receiving ration tickets

(Courtesy National Archives)

trader to trader, and the traffic in contraband liquor, arms and ammunition flourished.

Generally these traders were opposed to the concentration of Apaches and Navajos — two tribes that had always been profitable sources of barter — upon the Bosque Redondo reservation. The strict army surveillance about the forty-square miles made it impossible for the wandering merchants to carry their wares to these Indians. Only by keeping the Comanches and their cohorts, the Kiowas, stirred up could these men hope to gain their ends.

Carleton had sanctioned Navajo forays onto the Llano Estacado in search of livestock after the 1864-65 crop failures. From that time until the reservation's termination in 1868, a continual stream of Indians left Bosque Redondo in search of Comanche and Kiowa ponies. Clearly, Carleton's solution to New Mexico's Indian troubles, by playing one tribe against another, was to hang over his head like a double edged sword. Whatever way Carleton swung, the only result was trouble for his reservation at Bosque Redondo.

The general had hoped that the Fort Sumner experiment would eradicate the Navajo raiding pattern. However, the war-raiding traits of the Diné lingered on, as it was channelled into ways more acceptable to the army. It can even be postulated that sanctioned raiding onto the Staked Plains served as an outlet for some of the aggressive behavior engendered by the stress of living a day-to-day existence on a reservation far removed from the Navajo's traditional land, and ridden with disease and starvation. Without this outlet, the younger members of the tribe could have turned their aggressions inward, upon themselves to a greater extent than what already has been observed.

Comanche raids upon Bosque Redondo increased in proportion to the number of traders operating among South Plains tribes, and as conditions deteriorated at the Navajo reservation. In January 1865 Carleton alerted commanders of Forts Bascom and Sumner to be on the lookout for raiding parties. Stockmen in the vicinity of these posts were also cautioned to move their animals to the west side of the Pecos. By spring Comanche raids were weekly occurences. It was during that period that these Plains Indians drew their first Navajo blood. With the killing of several Navajos, who were foraging for fire wood, the army explicitly warned tribesmen not to stray far from the sanctuary of Fort Sumner.

Raids of the Plains Indians began as forays conducted by small parties of not more than fifteen warriors. As months passed, however, these raids increased in daring and intensity. By 1866 parties of Comanches, numbering in the hundreds, were penetrating the confines of the Navajo reservation. On July 13 of that year, a war party of more than 100 Indians — and reported to contain Mexicans — attacked Navajo herds. This group apparently paused long enough to inform New Mexican herders nearby of their strategy: "they did not want to kill Americans or Mexicans, but they would kill every Navajo they could."

Retreat and finding sanctuary in rough terrain were the Navajos' best defense against their enemies. The guerrilla tactics of scattering and fleeing before superior numbers had been successfully employed by the Navajos against the governments of Spain and Mexico, and with varying degrees of success against Anglo-American military expeditions until the Carson campaign. But the Navajos were not in their familiar redrock country. They were restricted to forty-square miles of flat, desolate reservation, the terrain of which was more familiar to their adversaries. Their lack of knowledge of this new environment precluded any chance of employing tactics which they had so keenly developed in their vast country to the northwest. Now the Navajos were trapped like ducks upon a pond.

With unrelenting enemies prowling their reservation, it was little wonder that Navajos lived in constant fear. Murmurings to return to their traditional country daily grew louder. The receipts furnished by the commissary department at Fort Sumner reflected the fact that some Indians were attempting to flee their enemies. During March 1865, 9,022 Indians drew rations. From that time until year's end, monthly returns showed a sizeable decrease in Indian population.

Plagued by Comanche raiders, undernourished, ravaged by disease, the Navajos longed for their old country, and grasped at every opportunity that might bring freedom. The army was at first reluctant to admit that Navajos were heading home; in fact, it was denied. By May 1865 the desertions had increased to such a point that their concealment and denial was impossible. Chief commissary officer, Captain H. B. Bristol, reported upon completion of the April 30th count, a loss of about 900 Indians. These desertions were attributed to the poorer and ailing tribesmen attempting to return to their old country, where they believed their health could be restored.

By June more than a thousand Navajos had left, and many more were voicing a desire to return to their traditional homeland. Ganado Blanco and Barboncito had slipped away with their herds of horses and sheep, and during the remaining summer months of 1865 there was every indication that a mass exodus was being contemplated by the remaining Indians. The garrison at Fort Sumner was kept under constant alert, and pickets about the reservation were strengthened. Navajos, however, continued to slip quietly away — and the garrison at Fort Sumner was powerless to stop them. The military could only cover up and attempt to smooth over the fact that discontent among the Indians was beyond all control.

What with the disastrous crop failures, the soaring disease rate, and the fighting incursions by Plains Indians, the plight of the Navajos was only compounded during late 1866 and into the early months of 1867. In fact, so loud was the discontent being voiced, that a special committee composed of officials from the Office of Indian Affairs journeyed to the reservation in June 1867 to confer first hand with the Indians. In council Navajo leaders were naively asked if they were satisfied with their reservation. Speaking for all the headmen present, Herrero Grande eloquently responded:

"We want to have the herds we had before we left our old country. And here we are hungry sometimes. We understand this was Comanche country, and their land. We are afraid our enemies will come here and steal our stock. We think the Comanches think this is their country and land, and they . . . have a right to come here and kill us and take our stock . . . The Comanches told me the lands belongs to them; the water belongs to them; the hunting grounds belongs to them; the wood belongs to them. And I believe it now, because they come here everyday and steal our stock. I think when our young men go out after wood, they won't come back again . . ., because our enemies are all around us.

"I am thinking more about my old country then ever before, because there I could secure myself from my enemies; here we have not that chance . . . We are all the time thinking of our old country, and we believe if the government will put us back they could have us the same there as here.

"I think the world, the earth, and in the heavens we are all equal and we have all been born by the same mother — what we want is to be sent back to our own country. Even if we starve there, we will have no complaints to make."

Navajo chiefs accused of counterfeiting ration tickets

(Courtesy National Archives)

Chapter Seven

THE CIVIL WAR years for New Mexico was a period of sharp conflict, not only militarily, but politically and economically as well. When it came to handling the Indian problem the normal gulf existing between political leaders became a virtual chasm. Prior to 1863 the Territory of New Mexico, as a political unit, had little to do with policy making relative to Indian affairs; the responsibility rested with the Federal Government and its military arm. As was natural, territorial leaders were ever alert to everything pertaining to the administration of Indian affairs which ran contrary to their vested interests. As Bosque Redondo was situated upon a large tract of land that had always been coveted by non-Indian settlers, the reservation — and Carleton's Indian policy — immediately became embroiled in controversy.

As William Keleher points out in *Turmoil in New Mexico*, livestock raisers resented the placement of Indians, whom they felt properly belonged to the recently created Territory of Arizona, upon a large area of the Pecos River Valley, depriving them of grazing rights on hundreds of thousands of acres of public domain. "This privilege they did not propose to forfeit without a terrific struggle."

From the very beginning the political opposition mustered against the Bosque Redondo experiment reflected the theme of grazing rights and public land. The actual situation, however, was soon blown far out of proportion in the struggle between military and civil authorities. The location of the Navajo Indians upon the Pecos River, "with at least two hundred thousand sheep" would surely deprive New Mexican stock men of invaluable land. Within months of the initial establishment of the reservation, the charge was being leveled that herders were being forced to move their animals to less desirable pasturage. Political tribunals resounded with the accusation that pillaging Indians were preferred to peaceful white citizens.

Inevitably James H. Carleton would face a day of reckoning. His military control over territorial affairs bordered on tyranny. He dictated curfews, editorial policies, economic programs, political platforms, and Indian affairs — all of which had been the domain of other governmental agents prior to the general's arrival in New Mexico. It was Carleton's autocratic Indian policy and his insuing battle with the superintendent of Indian Affairs which brought the Bosque Redondo experiment, once and for all, before legislators in Washington, D.C. — and set the stage for termination of the program.

Michael Steck, a physician by training, arrived in New Mexico from Pennsylvania in 1853 as Indian agent for the Mescalero Apaches. After ten years of labor among these Indians at the God-forsaken post of Fort Stanton, Steck succeeded the cantankerous James L. Collins as Superintendent of Indian Affairs for New Mexico in July 1863. Interestingly enough, both Steck and Carleton had similar views for handling New Mexico's Indian problems. They both saw that the time was near at hand when the government would be obliged to either feed the Indian or exterminate him; and that the white man's eternal search for precious metals would surely result in the latter, unless steps were taken to remove the Indian. Adoptation of the reservation system was the ultimate answer. Like Carleton, Steck believed that the Indian could be civilized and made self-sufficient. But complete eradication of tribal traditions — superstitions the superintendent called them — would first have to be accomplished before headway could be made in settling the Indians upon reservations. Indeed, both men sung the same song when it came to voicing a solution to the West's Indian problems. The only difference between the two, was that Steck was a practical man and accepted the limitations of the red man and of nature.

In October 1863 Michael Steck made his first visit to Bosque Redondo. After observing conditions at the post and speaking with both Apache and Navajo leaders, he confessed to Carleton that he approved "most cordially" of the policy being pursued. The Navajos, Steck pointed out to the Commissioner of Indian Affairs, "by their acts of wholesale destruction of life and property, and the general disregard they have exhibited of all former promises, have rendered themselves liable to severe punishment. The force now in the field, it is hoped, will be able to convey to them some practical lessons of the power of the government." Furthermore, Steck expressed the opinion that Bosque Redondo was the "only suitable place in New Mexico for a large Indian reservation." The superintendent, however, must have inwardly doubted the reservation's ability to maintain large numbers of Indians, for on his return to Santa Fe, he requested the opinion of John A. Clark, Surveyor General of New Mexico, as to the amount of arable land at the forty-square mile reserve. Surveyor General Clark's letter of reply substantiated Steck's fears:

> In reply to your enquiry, as to how much arable land would be included in a limit forty miles square — Fort Sumner . . . being the center. I have to state that the public surveys in this district have [not] been extended over the country described, and the only positive information I have, in relation to the character of the land in question, I derived from personal observation during a visit to Fort Sumner in the month of March last. I was on and along the Pecos River for a distance of seven or eight miles above and below the Fort and estimated the arable land within that distance at 4,000 acres. . . .

Surveyor General Clark's letter did much to shape the future attitude and actions of Michael Steck. In November the superintendent journeyed to Washington D.C., where he conferred with Bureau of Interior officials. During his visit to the capital, Steck changed his tune regarding the Indian policy being pursued by the army in New Mexico. He now made a rapid about-face and openly criticized the actions of General Carleton. On December 10 he wrote to Commissioner William P. Dole, expressing his true feelings about settling a large number of Indians upon the Pecos:

> . . . regard the location of [Bosque Redondo] as one of the best that could be made in New Mexico for a limited number of Indians. In the language of General Carleton, "the

Bosque Redondo is far down the Pecos in the open plain where these Indians can have no lateral contact with set-tlers." This the Hon. Commissioner is aware would be an important consideration in the selection of a permanent home for the Indians. East and west of the Bosque, no settle-ment can be made for the distance of seventy-five miles, be-ing arid plains, north the nearest settlement is 45 miles, and south it is not probable permanent settlement will ever be made as the salt plains in that direction render the water of the Pecos unfit for use.

While Steck concurred with the selection of Bosque Re-dondo for a reservation for a "limited number" of Indians, he doubted the site's ability to sustain a large Indian popula-tion.

"I beg leave to differ with Carleton," wrote the Superin-tendent to his superiors in Washington, "as to the practica-bility of removing and settling the Navajos upon it, for the following reasons. First, the arable land in the valley is not sufficient for both tribes; and secondary, it would be diffi-cult to manage two powerful tribes upon the same reserva-tion. This reserve as proposed is within the country claimed by the Apaches and to remove the bands, viz.: Jicarilla, Mescalero and Mimbres upon it, and divide the bands so as to give each family a farm large enough to eventually enable them to maintain themselves will occupy the whole valley. From my own observation upon a recent visit I am of opinion that 6,000 acres is a fair estimate of the amount of land susceptible of cultivation. This is also the opinion of John A. Clark, Surveyor General of New Mexico. . . . The three bands of Apaches will number at least 2,500 souls, and allowing five to a family and dividing the arable land equally

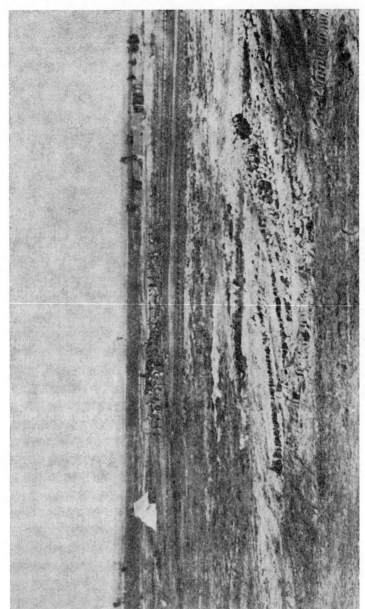

Adobe brickyard at Fort Sumner

would give each family . . . about twelve acres — an amount quite small enough to maintain them.

The Navajos it is well known number about 10,000. . . . If you take into account further that they own thousands of horses, and not less than 500,000 sheep, the impracticability of locating them upon a reservation of forty miles square, with 6,000 acres of arable land or even double that amount is so apparent that I need offer no arguments to prove it."

Thus Superintendent Steck endeavored to point out to the Commissioner of Indian Affairs the physical impossibility of locating all of New Mexico's Athapascan-speaking peoples upon the Bosque Redondo. He foresaw conflicts which would inevitably result, when the Mescaleros, a Plains-oriented tribe, were confined to the same reservation with Navajos, a semi-sedentary and far more numerous people. Steck diligently urged the Office of Indian Affairs to consider adoption of two separate reservations: one for Apaches at Bosque Redondo; and the selection of an adequate reserve for Navajos in their own country.

When news of Steck's sudden opposition to Bosque Redondo reached Carleton, the general was aghast. A few months previous both men had met at Fort Union and had, to all outward appearance, departed in total agreement with the policy being pursued. In an attempt to protect his moves and justify his actions, Carleton wrote to Adjutant General Lorenzo Thomas on January 12, 1864, stating that his plan for establishment of the reservation was unanimously endorsed by the legislature, late superintendent of Indian Affairs James Collins, Kit Carson and even Doctor Michael Steck — in short, "every intelligent man in the country approves it."

As far as the quantity of arable land at the reservation, Thomas was informed that there was more than enough in the immediate area. Even if there wasn't, added Carleton, land at Bosque Grande, twenty-five miles further down the river, could be used. Carleton believed that if Steck successfully thwarted his plans, it would be most unfortunate for New Mexico. The great thoroughfare over the 35th Parallel would be interrupted; those imaginary gold fields which Carleton constantly harped about, could not be worked; and the Navajo wars would continue for the next twenty years.

The evidence presented by Michael Steck did its job in Washington D.C. Carleton's hope for approval of his re-settlement program, and eventual support of Navajos by the Indian Department, had been shattered. On March 4 Commissioner William P. Dole informed Secretary of the Interior, J. P. Usher, of the points against settling Apaches and Navajos together on the same reservation; and advised the Department of the Interior not to assume responsibility for Navajos at that time. The army would continue to administer affairs of those Indians settled upon the Pecos River; and the gulf would continue to widen between Carleton and representatives of the Office of Indian Affairs in New Mexico — as the latter opposed the general's every move to force Navajos onto the forty-square mile reserve originally alloted to the Apaches.

By mid-May Carleton and Governor Henry Connelly were convinced that the major portion of the Navajos had surrendered, and those remaining in their old country were too few to cause any trouble. Accordingly, a proclamation was issued announcing "a suspension of arms in the prose-

cution of the war against the Navajo tribe." Thereafter all
forays by citizens against tribesmen remaining in Navajoland would be prohibited.

Although the war had officially closed, Indian depredations continued at an alarming rate. Needless to say, they
were always laid to the machinations of Navajo marauders,
whom it was claimed, still remained in large numbers in
their redrock sanctuaries. The same week that Connelly's
proclamation was issued, Ute Agent José Mansanarez, informed Michael Steck of alleged Navajo depredations
against citizens of Tierra Amarilla. The agent also related
that a party of New Mexicans had, a few weeks previous,
conducted a reprisal expedition against the Indians. This
party, according to Mansanarez, penetrated beyond the
Hopi villages in seach of captives and booty. However,
they soon regretted having done so, for they found themselves surrounded by over 200 mounted Navajos. The expedition finally fought their way out of the trap after killing
eighteen Indians. This account and the postscript which
Mansanarez added, gave every indication that Navajoland
was still very much alive with hostiles:

> I have been informed by various members of one of the ex-
> peditions against the Navajos which were out during the
> months of February, March and April, that they believe that
> a majority of the hostile Navajo warriors are still in their
> country.

This letter added fuel to Steck's opposition to "Fair Carletonia" — as Bosque Redondo was beginning to be contemptuously called. In another letter to Commissioner Dole,
the superintendent took the liberty to attack the assertions
of Carleton supporters, who claimed that few Navajos re-

mained in their old country. He claimed that facts of the case pointed to a completely different viewpoint. The tribe, contended the superintendent, was not anywhere near subdued; and the vast majority of its warriors were still in their own country. Those already at Bosque Redondo were of the poorer class who had willingly surrendered upon promise of food. The rich and by far the most powerful portion of the tribe remained where they always had been. As proof of this, Steck enclosed Mansanarez' letter and informed the commissioner of what he had been told by a delegation of Hopis now at the superintendency. This group of puebloans, alleged Steck, had reported "that the wealth and power of the Navajos had scarcely been touched."

To Michael Steck this was proof enough. It would be impossible to remove so large at tribe as the Navajos — and to attempt to would only result in immense costs to the government. Those Navajos already at Bosque Redondo, insisted Steck, were being fed at a rate of at least $50,000 monthly, and if the number of Indians were doubled — as surely they would be if the whole tribe were rounded up — supplies could not be furnished by a territory that was already being drained dry by military needs and martial law.

The picture painted by Superintendent Steck was gloomy but true. Carleton believed that the Navajos numbered no more than 8,000 — which the army could easily maintain at Bosque Redondo on short rations until crops matured. Major Henry Wallen, however, had found through experience that feeding even 6,000 was extremely difficult. Since inception of the roundup, Indian rations had been but a pound of breadstuffs per day for every man, woman and child — an amount that Carleton deemed quite sufficient.

Yet many Navajos appeared undernourished and deaths from malnutrition among infants and children were common.

The dire straits which "Fair Carletonia" was now in gave its opponents ammunition in their battle against the military authorities of New Mexico. During summer of 1864 the Santa Fe *New Mexican* began to change its tune. This newspaper's praise for Carleton and his Indian policy diminished. Instead, accounts of alleged Navajo outrages filled its pages. In all likelihood, Navajo depredations were continuing and were probably at an all time high. Carleton was charged repeatedly with being "too lenient" in his policy. Parroting Superintendent Michael Steck, the *New Mexican* contended that interests of the territory demanded Navajos be located west of the continental divide, upon the Little Colorado or Rio San Juan in their own country — instead of upon the Pecos. On October 28 the paper stated: "The white man should not be overlooked or his rights ignored, nor should every interest of the territory be permitted to suffer because one man has in opposition to the almost unanimous will of the people, conceived the idea of bringing the curse to their prosperity into our midst: making one of our most fertile valleys an asylum for the Indians of another territory; removing them from 300 to 400 miles east against the current of emigration and improvement . . ."

The fact that Navajos were not yet self-sufficient at Bosque Redondo was a vulnerable point of attack for the *New Mexican:* "They cannot be subsisted on less than one pound of beef and one pound of flour per day each. The cost of these two articles alone, delivered at the reservation, will be about forty cents. This sum multiplied by 8,000, and the product by 365, gives the nice little sum of $1,168,000. The Navajos themselves say that about one-half the tribe is at the Bosque . . .; remove the whole tribe, and the cost of feeding them will be . . . $2,336,000. . . ."

By late October 1864 Carleton was truely hard pressed. Crops had failed, civil authorities were pointing up his mistakes and appropriated Indian supplies had not reached New Mexico. It seemed as though every obstacle had been thrown in the path leading toward settlement of the Navajos. The Congressional bill appropriating $100,000 for clothing and maintenance of these people had passed on July 1 — as yet not a yard of cloth, blankets or spades had reached the territory. Carleton had received word that goods bought by these appropriations had left Fort Leavenworth on the first of October. With good luck they would be in New Mexico by December — just when the Navajos would need them most. In the meantime, 4,000 sheep purchased by the quartermaster department would have to furnish wool and meat for the cold and hungry Indians.

In accordance with instructions received in August, Michael Steck would proceed to Fort Union to meet the train of Indian goods. The superintendent would then personally accompany it to Fort Sumner, and there supervise its distribution to the Indians. By late November the goods had arrived in New Mexico. To forestall possibility of future disagreement, Brigadier General Crocker was cautioned by his superior to

afford Dr. Steck every assistance in your power to enable him to carry out the wishes of the Commissioner of Indian Affairs in the distribution of these goods . . . If the superintendent wishes to examine into the condition of the Indians under your charge and to go among and talk with them you will permit him to do so. . . .

These orders, however, were somewhat altered on December 9 when Assistant Adjutant General Benjamin C. Cutler informed the post commander that

about one year since, [when] Dr. Steck . . . went to the Bosque Redondo, he caused the Apaches to become discontented, by telling them that they could go to their own country to make mescal. If the doctor pursues any such course during his present visit, or talks with the Navajos in any manner to make them unhappy or discontented, he will be required at once to leave the reservation.

Following instructions, Steck proceeded to Fort Union; and on December 11 took custody of the wagon train of Indian goods. By January 1 he had arrived at the Bosque and the train load of blankets, shoes, tools and beads had been distributed to the Indians. The accompanying cattle, which were scheduled to be slaughtered as food for Navajos and Apaches, were turned out to graze and fatten first. In all, Steck spent four days quietly examining the reservation. He prudently reserved comment until he returned to Santa Fe. Once back in the capital, however, the superintendent took the liberty of reporting to the Commissioner of Indian Affairs, that he was "more than ever satisfied that the reservation at Fort Sumner will be a failure for so large a number of Indians. The Navajos are now leaving in small parties. They are all dissatisfied and can only be kept upon the Pecos by force. . . .

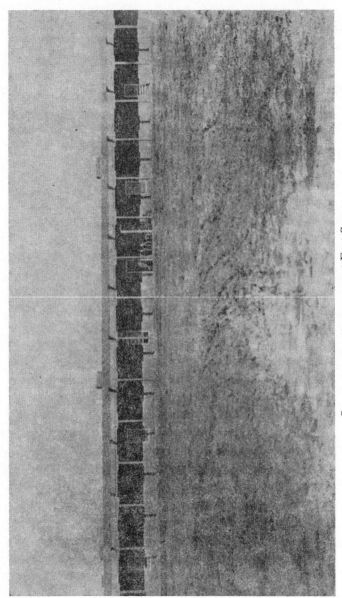

Quartermaster storerooms at Fort Sumner

(*Courtesy National Archives*)

The Indian goods delivered to Fort Sumner by Doctor Michael Steck, were carefully inspected by army personnel. By Special Order Number 133 (Dated December 20, 1864), a board of officers was authorized to be present at the distribution; and to witness the manner in which the annuities were passed out. Three days later the board had examined and counted the contents of the wagon train.

The board of inquiry found that many articles purchased from the appropriation were, in its opinion, of no use to the Indians; and many articles were purchased at prices which hinted — "that the purchasers were either culpably negligent, or entirely regardless of the interests of the Government and of the Indians." Blankets, for example, were bought at an average price of $18.50 per pair by the Office of Indian Affairs, while those purchased by ordnance and quartermaster departments were furnished at $5.85 per pair — and the latter were as good, if not superior to blankets purchased for the Indians. The officers believed that equally extravagant prices were paid for other items, but this could not be positively determined at the time.

From data collected the board concluded that between $30,000 to $40,000 would have covered the cost of all Indian goods distributed by Superintendent Steck. Concluding the inspection, the officers submitted their reports to General Carleton. By mid-January the department commander had read the papers: and they were again forwarded — this time to his superiors in Washington with following notation:

If, general, this is to be considered as a specimen of the manner in which the intentions of Congress in making appropriations are to be carried into practical effect, it would be well for that honorable body, when considering the matter with reference to how much of that appropriation would reach that point aimed at by them, to leave a wide margin for what in traget practice is technically called the "drift."

As these reports would inevitably cast unfavorable light upon the Office of Indian Affairs, Doctor Steck attempted to counter the charges. On February 15, 1865, he sent copies of board's report — *with comments* — to Commissioner Dole, so that the latter could "draw his own conclusions." Steck insisted the reports were "full of errors calculated to deceive, and no doubt intended to reflect upon the Indian Department." The superintendent maintained that the estimates were carelessly made — without the data necessary to assemble an impartial report. The blankets, Steck defended, were purchased in the east where prices were considerably higher; and that the inspection estimates were based on examination of little more than half of the articles actually purchased.

The dispute over the December deliverance of Indian goods resulted in final severance of cooperation — whatever little existed — between the Office of Indian Affairs and the military in New Mexico. The gradual buildup of mutual grievances which had existed for more than a year finally came to a head with expulsion of Mescalero Agent, Lorenzo Labadie, from the Fort Sumner reservation, a month after the board's report was forwarded to Washington.

Since Bosque Redondo had always been under strict control of the military, the feeble power of the Indian Office could be superseded at any time by the commanding officer, and the actions of its agent at Bosque Redondo were closely scrutinized by the army. With arrival of the first Navajos at

Fort Sumner, land which had been cleared by Mescalero Apaches was turned over to the intruders — much to the dismay and alarm of Agent Labadie. The Apache agent endeavored to induce Navajos to move off the ground that he felt properly belonged to his charges, but to no avail. Labadie's attempt to retain what little his charges had been alloted only brought suspicion from the army. In March 1864 Major Henry Wallen informed Carleton that the agent was "making the Navajos unhappy" by attempting to persuade them to move. The department commander issued instructions to watch Labadie's actions closely. Should the Mescalero agent continue to spread discontent among the Navajos, he would be ordered off the reservation.

From the first instance of conflict between Labadie and the army, matters grew worse. In months to come correspondence between Carleton and the post commander hinted of a definite plot afoot to oust the agent from the reservation. The agent's large flock of sheep grazing within reservation limits, to which he occasionally added to by purchasing animals from the Indians, was first to fall under the prying eyes of the military. On September 12 General Carleton directed Captain H. B. Bristol to investigate the matter; and to notify the agent that he could no longer graze within the area controlled by the army. Furthermore, the agent would not be permitted to purchase "an ounce of food from the Indians, nor under any circumstances a single sheep."

While the Apache agent's grazing rights were being restricted, his duties as administrator of 400 Indians was being closely scrutinized. More than six months previous, Kit Carson, while supervising Navajo labor, remarked about the apparent lack of progress which Apaches were making

When questioned about his cargo, Labadie frankly admitted that these articles were not his, but were obtained illegally from Captain Calloway, Superintendent of the Navajo farms. Furthermore, the agent revealed that he had negotiated the purchase of government cattle from quartermaster officer, Captain Prince G. Morton. A subsequent investigation revealed seventy-five head of cattle with U. S. brands in the agent's herd grazing outside the limits of military control. Lorenzo Labadie had been caught redhanded in theft and fraud. On March 22 a court martial was convened to hear charges against the officers and the agent. Both Captains Calloway and Morton were found guilty and dismissed from service. As Labadie was a civilian, and thus not subject to the discipline of the military courts, he was ordered to promptly leave the Bosque Redondo.

With termination of the Civil War the nation could once again turn from problems of a strictly military nature to those facing the country as a whole. Turmoil stemming from maltreatment of the American Indian now pressed for attention. In Washington there was growing suspicion that many Indian wars were provoked by "aggressions of lawless white men;" that the number of red men were growing steadily less due to disease, "cruel treatment on the part of the whites — both by irresponsible persons and by government officials;" and by the ever increasing encroachments of the westward movement upon domain of the red man.

On March 3, 1865, a Joint Special Committee composed of members of both houses of Congress was appointed to inquire into these conditions. The work which this committee undertook was so immense — covering the problems of a continent — that holding of regular hearings, were in many cases, impossible. Instead, a circulating letter was sent to regular army officers, Indian agents, inquiring into their knowledge of Indian affairs.

This Special Committee was split into three divisions; and its chairman, James R. Doolittle of Wisconsin, Vice President of the United States, Lafayette S. Foster, and Lewis W. Ross of Illinois, were assigned New Mexico, Utah, Colorado, Indian Territory and the state of Kansas. This portion of the committee began its work at Fort Leavenworth on May 17; and by July 4 its investigations had been extended to New Mexico. The hearing in Santa Fe, and a cursory inspection of the Bosque Redondo reservation, revealed the depth of New Mexican Indian troubles. The horrors of the Navajo roundup and the tribe's subsequent imprisonment upon the Pecos River reservation would be the prime issue under investigation. Out of the mass of conflicting testimony and reports came one thread of truth — that the tribe was suffering from the ravages of disease and malnutrition; that their stock was nearly gone, as was their pitiful reserve of fuel.

The multiple reasons contributing to the failure of Bosque Redondo were analyzed. From officials of the Indian Department, military, the clergy, and business, social, and political leaders came a flood of testimony indicating the existence of a virtual war of attrition between the Indians and the New Mexicans. Navajo women and children were fair-game to slavers and procurers as much as Mexican livestock was to the Navajos. As the state of affairs stood, complete removal of the tribe was inevitable. But aspects of this removal shocked the Doolittle Committee. Not only was the Navajo campaign conducted in a brutally harsh manner — which certainly was necessary from a military standpoint — but transferral of the Indians to the Bosque Redondo was carried out with all the feelings of a cattle drive. What was more tragic was that the ultimate destination of these Indians had been an unfortunate choice.

Doolittle and his colleagues saw that the soil at Fort Sumner was impregnated with alkali, and the high mineral content of the Pecos induced dysentery among the Indians. No matter how hard the government endeavored to settle Navajos on a reservation, away from their old country, and instruct them in the white man's ways, it would never succeed. Although Navajos had always been highly adaptive, they fought with tooth and nail those plans which would change basic traits of the tribe. They accepted only what ideas they could profitably use and rejected all others.

To all outward appearances there were no immediate improvements brought by the Doolittle Committee. When once back in Washington, the Committee began the tedious task of sifting through the mass of collected data. To make its investigation even more thorough, and thus give a clearer insight into problems facing the Navajos, the committee requested the Department of the Interior to undertake an investigation of its own. Therefore in late 1865 the Office of Indian Affairs authorized Special Agent Julius K. Graves to investigate New Mexican affairs, prior to an anticipated takeover of the Fort Sumner reservation by civil authorities.

Upon reaching New Mexico in December 1865, Graves "found the Indian question the all absorbing topic of conversation." The main controversy revolved around the selection of Bosque Redondo as a permanent home for Navajos. The special agent soon found that feeling ran so high among the populace that political parties were being styled as "Bosque" or "anti-Bosque." Graves reported that the whole territory was politically split over the reservation: many favored it, others opposed the policy as being detrimental to the interests of New Mexico; and the entire matter seemed to drift off into a question of political expediency.

Not knowing what to believe, the special agent journeyed to Bosque Redondo to investigate firsthand the source of conflict. On December 31 Navajo headmen were summoned to an interview; and for more than six hours these Indians poured out their woes. With their usual dignity the headmen payed deep attention to the entire proceeding; and took a keen interest in everything that the representative of the Indian Office had to say. Graves explained that he had been sent to their reservation to see if they were well fed and properly cared for. He earnestly tried to impress upon the headmen that the only way he could find answers to his questions was for them, one by one, to tell him of their wishes, and the problems facing their people.

When their turn came to speak, the language of each headman was plain and practical, and their allusions and illustrations truly eloquent and appropriate. In speaking, they expressed their sentiments as only Navajo orators can.

"This is the best place for us we know of outside of our country. We want to go back to that country. We have done wrong but we have learned better and if allowed to return to our mountain homes, we will behave ourselves well.

"If the government wants us to remain here we will do so and do the best we can — but we cannot be as contented as we would be in our old homes — we shall think of them — we all do think of them. There is something within us which does not speak but thinks — and though we remain silent, our faces speak to each other.

"Cage the badger and he will try to break from his prison and regain his native hole. Chain the eagle to the ground — and he will strive to gain his freedom, and though he fails, he will lift his head and look up to the sky which is home — and we want to return to our mountains and plains, where we used to plant corn, wheat and beans."

Although Graves conceded that General Carleton's policy was having an "excellent effect," he nevertheless suggested that the government should, once and for all, put an end to the quarrels among civil and military authorities in New Mexico. It must decide whether or not Navajos were going to be permanently retained at Bosque Redondo, and necessary appropriations provided to adequately care for them. The existing jurisdiction — rationed by the army, and clothed by the $100,000 annually appropriated by Congress — only created animosities between the two branches of government. Graves felt that either the Navajos should be supported and educated by the military, or they should be turned over to civil authorities.

Despite Graves' suggestions, the controversy appeared as if it would never be resolved. Few men dared to attack Carleton and his death-like grip over the territory. Doctor Michael Steck had grown tired of matching wits and resigned as Superintendent of Indian Affairs on May 1, 1865, as he stated — "for the good of the service." Felipe Delgado filled the remainder of Steck's term until replaced by the appointment of A. Baldwin Norton, of Ohio, on February 17, 1866.

The new superintendent gave Bosque Redondo a cusory inspection, and then sat down and wrote his superiors in Washington that the whole experiment would prove a failure, for "the soil is cold, and the alkali in the water destroys it." The tragic failure of the 1866 crop substantiated the superintendent's prophesy. In fact, the Indian population was totally demoralized. They had experienced one failure after another, and had witnessed like failures on the part of their military overseers. The brackish water brought dysentry, and the garrison syphilis and gonorrhea. Only the menacing guns of the army prevented a mass decampment that year.

Chapter Eight

THE INVESTIGATIONS of the Doolittle Committee transformed the Bosque Redondo controversy from purely a local irritation to that of a national issue. Try as it might, the army was powerless to hide the fact that this reservation was little more than a concentration camp, and that it had been the brain-child of one man — General James H. Carleton — born of military and economic expediency and sustained by New England tenacity. The Civil War, however, had ended and the nation clamored for return to some semblance of sanity, and many duties which had been the sole responsibility of the military were now being transferred back to civil hands. Slowly churning, the wheels of government began to take up the issues of Indian affairs in the far Southwest, and forever seal the fate of the Bosque Redondo experiment.

Before the Office of Indian Affairs could act upon the Navajo issue it first had to know precisely what it was stepping into. With that in view, the Secretary of the Interior James Harlan, requested the War Department to present reports as to the exact costs of subsisting the Indians at Bosque Redondo. Through the chain of command, these requests trickled, finally reaching James Carleton in New Mexico. Hesitantly, the commander issued orders authorizing an exact inventory of all equipment, livestock, and produce on hand at the reservation. By end of 1865 the tabulations were on their way to Washington, D.C. — all revealing the tremendous costs at which the tribesmen were being sustained.

After careful study of these papers, Harlan found that for an eighteen month period (March 1, 1864 to October 1, 1865) $1,114,981.70 had been expended just to feed the Indians alone. The reports, with their staggering costs, were then passed on to the Commission of Indian Affairs, D. N. Cooley, for any consideration and recommendations the latter might wish to make. In the meantime, Harlan played for time by informing the Secretary of War, that his department "would cheerfully undertake the duty of supplying these Indians as soon as Congress shall provide the necessary means."

General James Carleton realized that he was now treading on shaky ground. There was every possibility that control of Bosque Redondo would pass from his hands into those of the Department of the Interior, and hence, into the hands of the Office of Indian Affairs — with whose representatives he had for years waged a running battle. Such a move would signal the complete defeat of his "Indian policy." Again the general pleaded for his reservation — this time for continued patronage from the Department of War:

> I beg to express the opinion that the whole of this matter of purchasing food, etc., for the Indians, and of issuing the articles thus purchased to the Indians, as well as the direction of their labor, until they are more civilized be left in the

hands of the War Department. I know and have so written, that to do this will impose a burden upon the military not properly belonging to them . . ., but experience and observation compel me to say that if this matter passes out of the hands which hold the power there will be complications, embarrassment, misunderstanding, etc., which will result, I fear in great injury to, if not in the positive failure of the important measure of fixing forever the Navajo tribe of Indians upon a reservation.

This matter, however, was now out of Carleton's hands. In fact, his career as commander of the Department of New Mexico was also fast approaching an end. During fall of 1865 New Mexican politicans were actively campaigning to obtain his removal. Expert in Machiavellistic art, the anti-Carleton faction maneuvered their fight into the Territorial Assembly. Although it could do nothing directly to obtain the general's removal, the assembly could accelerate it by resorting to the traditional New Mexican custom of adopting a memorial, professing to reflect the people's sentiments. As the Carleton controversy gained momentum, routine legislative matters became secondary. After much debate — and possibly some bribery — the memorial was finally adopted on January 21, 1866, by a vote of 9 to 2 in the Council, and 20 to 4 in the House. The document was personally addressed to President Andrew Johnson, and urged "that a more capable officer be sent to command the troops immediately." The memorial stated that Carleton had failed in all attempts to subdue the Indians; and that the large military forces stationed throughout the territory were providing a lucrative business for army contractors and sutlers. The legislators also charged that Carleton, instead of pursuing Indian raiders as was his duty, had actually blamed depredations upon New Mexicans.

The legislative memorial did its job. On September 19, 1866, the Secretary of War directed the commander of the Department of the Missouri to relieve James H. Carleton from duty in New Mexico and order him to report to duty with his regiment (the Fourth Cavalry) in the Department of the Gulf.

After four years of high drama, James Henry Carleton's military career had ignaminously ended. Entering the territory on August 7, 1862, at the head of 1,500 California Volunteers, "to drive the Texans from New Mexico," the general was immediately welcomed as the savior of New Mexico. As William Keleher points out, the fortunes of the times dictated Carleton's success. "In almost any other theatre of war Carleton would probably have won honor and renown similar to that achieved elsewhere by major officers of his rank and experience. With hundreds of soldiers marking time, demanding action in the war, Carleton blundered into a campaign against the Apaches and Navajos, and conducted it with results that were disastrous to the Indians, and unfortunate for the government. No doubt but that Carleton was in authority in New Mexico at a time when unusual and extraordinary conditions pravailed. People blamed him for almost every adverse happening in the territory between the time of his arrival and departure. When beef and flour sold for twenty dollars the hundred in 1864, the near starving civilian population blamed Carleton because he used government gold to outbid them in buying supplies for the army and the Indians. When the Indians raided the settlements, the people criticized Carleton for failure to prevent the raids, and for not following the raiders and killing them. When Carleton's troops shot and killed Apaches and Navajos, some New Mexican citizens called him a barbarian and a cold blooded murderer. When Carleton rounded up the Navajos, showing no mercy, and imprisoned them at Bosque Redondo, some New Mexican politicians accused him of high crimes and misdemeanors, not because of his treatment of the Indians, but because it was believed the Indians would be settled on public domain that had been used by the white settlers rent-free as grazing and breeding grounds since the days of the Spanish conquest."

The final repudiation of General Carleton's policy came within four months of his transferral. On December 31, 1866, Secretary of War U. S. Grant authorized issuance of Special Orders Number 651, directing the commander of the Department of the Missouri to give "immediate orders to turn over the control of the Navajo Indians . . . to such agents of the Indian Department as may be . . . designated to receive and take charge of them." In accordance with General Grant's dictum another order was issued twelve days later which reiterated the instructions, and listed additional ones preparatory to relinquishment of military control. An "accurate detailed inventory," or census, would first be taken of all Navajo captives. The commander of the Department of New Mexico was instructed to give whatever military assistance to the Indian agent as may be deemed necessary — "but without going beyond the strict duties and administration of the military service, or interfering with . . . the Indian Department." Finally, authority was granted the Indian Department to make requisitions

Company quarters at Fort Sumner, 1864

(Courtesy National Archives)

upon army subsistence and quartermaster departments for feeding the Navajos.

Although orders authorizing transfer of the Navajo reservation to civil control had been made public, the Bosque Redondo reservation was snarled in government red tape, and orders were exceedingly slow in reaching New Mexico. The Superintendent of the Territory, A. Baldwin Norton, and Theodore Dodd, the resident agent for the Navajos, could not take charge of 7,000 Indians until they had concrete instructions. To make matters worse, adequate appropriations for subsisting the Indians had not been passed by Congress for the fiscal year 1867-68. Only the usual $100,000 had been approved — scarcely enough to feed the Navajos. "The idea of trying to subsist them (7,400 Navajos) for one year for $100,000 is ridiculous," wrote Dodd in disgust. "This cannot be done for less than $400,000; the government must either continue to feed them or turn them loose. . . ."

While politicians and military officials dragged their heels in Washington, the Navajos continued to suffer upon their wretched reservation. Their sheep had dwindled to less than a thousand, and Comanches had driven off most of their horses and mules. The plight of the Navajos was desperate, and their discontented murmurings were loud. During July, Superintendent Norton journeyed to Fort Sumner to listen to their complaints. In council with Navajo leaders, he naively asked if they were satisfied with their reservation. As principal chief, Herrero eloquently expressed the innate fear of isolation which all Navajos feel, but which had been blown out of proportion by the extreme conditions at Bosque Redondo.

"We want to have the herds we had before we left our old country," lamented the chief. Here we are hungry sometimes. We understand that this was Comanche country, and their land. We are afraid our enemies will come here and kill us and steal our stock. We think the Comanches think this is their country and land, and they . . . have a right to come here and kill us and take our stock . . . The Comanches told me the land belongs to them. The water belonged to them. The hunting grounds belonged to them. The wood belonged to them. And I believe it now, because they (the Comanches) come here everyday and steal our stock. I think when our young men go out after wood, they won't come back again . . ., because our enemies are all around us.

"I am thinking more about my old country than ever before, because there I could secure myself from my enemies; here we have not that chance. . . . We are all the time thinking of our old country, and we believe if the government will put us back they could have us the same there as here.

"Notwithstanding the cold and heat we have worked and we will work, but poor as we are we would rather go back to our country. What does the government want us to do. More than we have done? Or more than we are doing?

"What we want is to be sent back to our own country. Even if we starve there, we will have no complaints to make."

A week after Norton returned to Santa Fe, word reached him from the Department of the Interior, directing him to assume control of the Indian prisoners. On August 21 he communicated with the new commander of the Department of New Mexico, General G. W. Getty, asking if the commander of Fort Sumner had been authorized to transfer the Navajos to Theodore Dodd, their resident agent at the reservation. Norton was stunned when he learned from Getty that "no such order had been received or issued."

Again the question of control over Bosque Redondo was being bantered around by both army and civil leaders, and the orders for relinquishment of control had been purposely held up. It had been eight months since the issuance of Special Orders Number 651. The slowness of the army was deliberate. The War Department demanded one more investigation of the Navajo situation, and this task was assigned to Lieutenant R. McDonald, of the Fifth Cavalry. His report, completed on November 12, 1867, again revealed conditions as they actually were. Without mincing words, McDonald recommended that the Navajos be removed "to a suitable location, where wood, water and grass abound." When the report reached Washington, however, the debate was narrowed to semantics, and the two words — "suitable location" — was focused upon. Commander of the Department of the Missouri, General William Tecumseh Sherman — who had never been in New Mexico — proposed locating the Navajos in Indian Territory, east of the 98th parallel; in fact, this latter proposal was being considered even while McDonald was making his survey. The Office of Indian Affairs, knowing the views of its officials in New Mexico, as well as those of territorial politicians, looked favorable upon returning the Navajos to their old country. By end of October 1867, the question had been resolved. The Indians would at last be transferred to civil control. All that remained was the drafting of the final orders of release, and that was not long in coming.

Early in 1868 Congress, long pressured by Indian rights advocates, as well as by members of the Doolittle committee, authorized steps be taken to iron out the existing difficulties with Indian tribes — and among these steps was the enactment of treaties. To carry out the wishes of Congress, a Peace Commission had been organized during the summer of 1867. When assembled this group was indeed a distinguished gathering: Senators J. B. Henderson, John B. Sanborn and Samuel Tappan represented the civil government; and Generals W. T. Sherman, Alfred H. Terry, William S. Harney and C. C. Auger upheld the military; and the whole was chairmaned by Commissioner of Indian Affairs, N. G. Taylor. Together these men would attempt to revolutionize the Indian service, and bring to an end many of the squabbles existing between red and white men.

The Peace Commission criticized the existing administration of Indian Affairs. It saw rampant corruption within the service, and requested congress to relieve all agents and special agents from duty by February 1, 1869 — "and replace them with men of reputable character and integrity." A revision of intercourse laws was urged, and the commission concluded that the practice, which had so long been in vogue, of appointing governors as *ex-officio* superintendents was detrimental to Indian affairs. The Peace Commission unanimously recommended that no more legislators be permitted to fill these positions. Also banned was the authority of state and local governments to call upon militia during Indian uprisings; and all regulations governing Indian trade would be placed under stringent control. The military would be vested with authority to eject, by force if necessary, all traders and intruders found upon Indian lands.

And finally, a treaty with the Navajos of New Mexico was advocated.

Lieutenant General William T. Sherman and Colonel Samuel F. Tappan were the peace commissioners appointed to negotiate the Navajo treaty. Arriving at Fort Sumner on May 28, the officials immediately began an inquiry into the plight of the Navajos. For two days they observed the miserable conditions at Bosque Redondo. Both men had arrived at the reservation determined to move the tribe further east, probably into Indian Territory. Their conference with Navajo headmen, however, soon convinced both that these Indians were unalterably opposed to being moved to any other place other than their old country. The Navajos, starving, diseased and homesick, were willing to agree to anything, so long as they would be granted their one desire. For three days Sherman and Tappan conferred with Indian leaders, represented principally by Delgadito, Barboncito, Manuelito, Largo, Armijo, and Torivo.

Although the commissioners recognized that the reservation was a failure, they had not made up their minds as to the best location for the Navajos. Sherman still clung to the idea of locating the tribe further east, in Indian Territory, while Tappan, who had served in Colorado during the Civil War, was somewhat in favor of leaving the Navajos in the Far West. The chiefs, all of whom had been reduced to poverty by their exile, wanted only to be returned to their redrock country. They knew that General Sherman had a complete and God-like control over their destiny. Desparately they would agree to anything that would bring freedom and restore to them a degree of dignity.

By May 29, the commissioners had been swayed enough. They would let the Navajos return to their traditional lands. But the bargain had yet to be driven setting the limits of the reservation. That came the next day, and it was anything but generous. The Navajos would be returned to a 3.5 million acre tract — a fraction of the 23 million acres they had claimed previous to their incarceration. On behalf of the government, a $150,000 would be made available for tribal rehabilitation, and 15,000 sheep and goats, and 500 cattle were promised in an effort to rebuild the Navajo's livestock resources. The treaty was officially consummated the following day — June 1, 1868 — by the commissioners representing the United States, and for the Navajos by a twelve-man council and a number of lesser chiefs. Nearly two months later — on July 25 — the document was ratified by the Senate and proclaimed by President Andrew Johnson on August 12, 1868.

Within two weeks of treaty signing, preparations had been completed for mass-removal of the Navajos from Fort Sumner. Quartermaster wagons stood ready, and livestock — all that remained of Navajo herds — was corralled for the long trek. At dawn, on June 18, 1868, ten miles long, a column left Fort Sumner under escort of four companies of cavalry. The long line, with its nearly 100 wagons, animals, and a mulititude of women and children moved slowly, covering only ten to twelve miles a day. Up the Pecos valley, through Anton Chico and Cañon Blanco they marched — along the route they had traveled to the Bosque Redondo four years previous. On July 4 Tijeras Cañon, twelve miles east of Albuquerque, was reached. The Navajos now knew that their country lay but a short distance away, and excitement gripped them. The next day they quietly forded the Rio Grande, and by the end of the month they had reached Fort Wingate.

Destitute of all sustaining things, and stripped of their status and dignity the once "Lords of New Mexico," as the Navajos had been described during their height of power, had come home.

Navajo brave at Fort Sumner
(*Courtesy Smithsonian Institution*)

Conclusion

FOLLOWING THEIR release from captivity the Navajos fought their way back to economic prosperity. By tenacity of purpose, fortitude and thrift, they overcame the innumerable vicissitudes of cultural reorientation. But the ordeal of what befell them burned within Navajo memories for generations. For the first time in 150 years of conflict, these Indians had been truly subdued. An effective plan of war had been devised, and carried out. The objective of Carleton's campaign had been simple — destroy the tribe's resources: lay waste to their corn fields, orchards, herds and flocks, burn their granaries, corrals and hogans; and immediate and effective were the results.

Never had the Navajos felt such destruction, and on such a large scale. They had no other choice but to surrender and be marched to their destination, nearly 400 miles away. Although Navajos speak of the rigors of being transported — during the dead of winter — to the Bosque Redondo, it was the four years of exile that they remember with sadness. In fact, the term "Long Walk," denoting the movement of Indians from Navajoland to Fort Sumner, is an Anglo-American fabrication. The term is not used among these Indians unless introduced by an outsider. In all probability, this term was coined for its dramatic appeal by early writers such as Washington Matthews, J. P. Dunn, or Thomas Rarish. The word *"Hwelte"* — a corruption of the Spanish word *fuerte*, meaning fort, is what the Navajos use when talking of this period in their history. Without exception, *Hwelte* refers to Fort Sumner, and does not include the transferral to the reservation.

The effects of these years of incarceration upon Navajo culture and personality were profound. Navajo reactions during this period, of course, varied with specific segments of this society and indicate the ways in which they coped with the stress so profoundly felt. Perhaps cooperation was the most visible reaction. Compliance with army dictates — almost bordering on blind submission — characterized the internment for the majority of Indians. Agricultural projects were undertaken without complaint for the most part, and brought to speedy conclusion with few tools. When rations were cut following crop failures there had been few murmurs. Navajos had always lived on the edge of starvation and cinching of the belt was nothing new. But when starvation resulted in death and general weakening, bringing disease, the reactions of these Indians drastically changed.

As the Bosque Redondo experiment wore on, year after year, conditions gradually degenerated at the reservation. Failure became the by-word of "Fair-Carletonia" — failure in agriculture, failure to protect the Indians from enemies, and failure to provide adequate shelter, fuel and clothing. Withdrawal and apathy became the characteristic symptom of this failure.

In conferences with military leaders and the representatives of the Office of Indian Affairs tribal headmen reiterated the feelings of their people — and those feelings rang with apathy, frustration, and eventual withdrawal. Perhaps the symptom of withdrawal is best exmplified in those speeches by Navajo headmen, which told of Navajo longings for their traditional land, and of the loneliness which they endured upon a reservation which was so distasteful and alien to them.

The mass removal of these people from their homeland, which was replete with shrines having sacred significance, greatly added to the feeling of uneasiness. Then, as today, sacred places are tremendously important to the Navajos, for these spots represent physical proof of their legendary heritage. The traditions that form the backbone for the complicated ceremonies always relate past events on or below this earth; and it is through these legends and rituals that Navajos know of the activities of the Holy Ones, which they venerate. Thus the numerous mountains, streams, springs, and cañons that are sacred to the tribe, serve to reinforce the validity of these supernatural personages; and in so doing, reinforce the very core of Navajo ritual patterns. "These features stand as monuments to the prowess of the Holy Ones," writes Frederick W. Sleight, "and above all, they are physical proof to the Navajos that all is as it should be. . . . Because of the unchanging character of these great features, a form of solidarity and security permeates Navajo society." But what happened when these Indians could no longer view their beloved shrines; could not reinforce tribal lore and tradition — as in the case of their removal? When curing rites failed many Navajos felt that a general impotency had befallen their lot, induced in no small measure by their isolation from sacred areas. Little wonder, therefore, that ailing tribesmen sought every means of leaving Bosque Redondo during 1866 and 1867. As sickness increased, defying not only the native practioners, but the military doctors as well, the feelings of futility and impotency likewise grew. The reactions became more unreasonable and pathological, venting themselves on scapegoats, through the media of rumors and intimidations of witchcraft. The Navajos were perceiving the stress and reacting to it through their system of beliefs.

Because they have deep connections "with the springs of man's existence," systems of beliefs are the most difficult of all man's institutions to change. "Systems of beliefs," wrote Alexander Leighton, "resembles a thick matting of roots under the floor of the forest which if cut may result in the withering of some distant bush or a whole tree. A man who intrudes into another culture, or way of life, with administrative acts may be like one who cuts bothersome roots without being aware of their functions and interconnections. The people of the other culture, however, like the trees of the forest, even if themselves ignorant of the functional nature of their systems of beliefs, nevertheless feel it when their roots are cut."

James Carleton's premise for establishing the Bosque Redondo reservation was to change the very core of Navajo beliefs — first by punishment, then by education and hard work. Groups of people, however, cannot effectively carry out acts for which they have no underlying systems of beliefs — and here is where Carleton blundered. The evidence points to the fact, that as times became harder at the reservation, and as the army imposed greater controls, creating greater stress, Navajo dependency on religious beliefs became greater. Withdrawal from army medical help and seeking of native medicine men was the immediate result; and the venting of rumors of witchcraft and suspicion and aggressive acts towards segments of the population, *viz.:* the Mescaleros and the Cebolleta Navajos, followed soon after.

While Carleton went to great lengths to learn the geography of Navajoland, prior to his campaign; he failed miserably to comprehend the geography of Navajo beliefs. Carleton grasped the basis for Navajos prestige, for he directed his field commanders to destroy those elements which tribal wealth was hinged to. But like his predecessors, Carleton did not comprehend the basis of Navajo authority; nor the beliefs relating to sickness, death, reward and punishment. Because of the general's blindness — which was the product of his time — nearly all his plans failed, with the exception of the building of agriculture projects.

Inseparably related to systems of beliefs, are the habits and customs whereby people interact with each other. Sociologists lump these together, and label them "social organization." The relationship between beliefs and social organization cannot be divided, for they interact together. Like the principle already outlined for systems of beliefs, it is impossible to force people to carry out actions for which they have no social organization. Carleton believes that a new governing body could be created for the Indians at Bosque Redondo — that democratic institutions could replace the hierarchy of prestige that was so much a part of

Navajo outlook — possession of wealth, skill in oratory, and physical ability in war.

Twelve leaders were selected from among the Apaches and Navajos; and the basis for picking these men were not so much premised on tribal preference, as upon the fact that these men catered to the military. They were puppets in the very real sense of the word. The Mescalero arrived with few leaders. Chief Manuelito and José Largo had been killed early in the roundup. Cadete and Ojo Blanco, while they were respected by their followers, were minor chiefs when they assumed charge of their people. Both, however, soon realized the intolerable situation, and led their people back to the traditional haunts in the Sacramento Mountains.

Prior to the Carson campaign, the social organization of the Navajo was weakly organized, with leadership divided among clan and band chieftains — no one headman actually speaking for the majority of the tribe. The military campaign and subsequent incarceration soon disrupted whatever cohesion existed. At Fort Sumner, with a population gathered from widely scattered areas, it is doubtful if any member of the chosen group of chiefs actually spoke for majority of the Navajo prisoners. What power they had, was derived from their responsibility for drawing rations for a selected number of tribesmen.

The Navajos came to Fort Sumner as strangers. All accustomed relationships with family, clan, band, and neighbors had been wiped away by Carson's campaign. As a people, they had never experienced confinement, and they baulked at the prospects of living like Pueblo Indians. Carleton was stymied in his attempt to force these Indians into close community relationships. And knowledgable Carson, was bewildered when the Navajos knocked the north walls out of the hogans upon the death of a family member, thus ruining the mountain man's attempts to settle these Indians in villages "with uniform streets." While religious beliefs and social structure defeated Carleton, he nevertheless attained a semblance of success with other forms of collective activity.

The Navajos were agriculturists, and unlike the Mescalero harbored no adversion to tilling the soil. They came to Fort Sumner possessing rudimentary knowledge of irrigation; and once supplied with tools their accomplishments were truly amazing. The irrigation system that they constructed was probably the most intricate and best engineered in all of New Mexico, and only the quirks of nature prevented the Bosque Redondo reservation from really blooming. Had it not been for droughts and worms, the reservation would have been self-sustaining within a year of its founding.

It is an infinitely long and complicated process for a group of people to acquire a new social organization. Carleton innately knew this, and was prepared for a long and hard battle when it came time to change basic Navajo drives. His unfortunate choice of site for the reservation, combined with turbulent political conditions in New Mexico, to preclude any chance of success. Even if the conditions had been right, it is doubtful if acculturation could have been possible on the scale envisioned by Carleton. The general sought eradication of Navajo raiding patterns and the establishment of democratic institutions. Only a humiliating defeat would bring the former, and the latter has been more than thirty years in formulation. Conditions at the Bosque

Redondo reservation only compounded the obstacles in the path to acculturation.

Physical discomfort, economic losses, restriction of movement, separation from family, rejection, dislike and suspicion deeply affected what social structure existed at the reservation. The constant battle between the military and the Office of Indian Affairs left the Indian with a feeling of confusion and mistrust. They did not know what to do, who to follow; and friction and disagreement between tribal segments were the natural consequence. Petty factions appeared, as individuals struggled to assert their identity and gain power and prestige. Navajo bucks who were gifted enough to rob the army and the Mescaleros without being caught, soon found themselves with considerable following. Curers and singers were fortunate enough to appear as heelers on a reservation ridden with disease, soon had prestige and wealth beyond their wildest dreams. Their status and hold over their people resulted in uneasy feelings on the part of the army. So too, those leaders appointed by the army commanded allegiance by their ability to call the shots respecting allotment of rations and gifts.

Each of these reactions demonstrated the manner by which Navajos sought to meet the stresses which premeated the reservation. The chiefs appointed by the army were cooperative, and sought to keep the reservation running on even-keel. The medicine man withdrew from any relationship with the military, seeking instead the answers to their confusion and the bewilderment of their people in the imbalance of nature and the machinations of witches and shadowy personages. The *ladrones* reacted aggressively, attacking and stealing; and soon a situation developed with three groups completely at odds with one another; and complete disarticulation was the inevitable result. With the disruption of leadership, or working relationships, people become less able to protect themselves from physical discomforts, threats to health and life — uncertainties and frustrations are soon multiplied. In short, social disorganization tends to increase the stress already present in the community. It took nearly three years to reach the breaking point at Bosque Redondo. By late 1866 Navajos were leaving the reservation in large numbers, and those remaining were beaten to a point where apathy, and blind submission was the common state at Bosque Redondo. What Sherman and Tappan found at Fort Sumner were the hulks of a once proud people. The removement of the Navajos, as viewed by the peace commissioners would accept any compromise so long as they were removed from "Fair Carletonia." As one old Navajo once voiced. "We had been beaten to the ground. Smashed to little pieces like clods. We had learned what captivity and poverty did to our people."

Bibliography

Bibliography

ARCHIVAL COLLECTIONS

U. S. National Archives, War Records Division and
Indian Affairs Records Division

Fort Canby Post Returns, 1864, Record Group 94.

Fort Craig Post Returns, 1864-68; Record Group 94.

Fort Defiance Post Returns, 1851-1861, Record Group 94.

Fort Fauntleroy Post Returns, 1860-61; Record Group 94.

Fort Lyon Post Returns, 1862; Record Group 94.

Records of the Office of Adjutant General, Record Group 94, Letters Received from Department of New Mexico, 1860-1870.

Records of the Office of the Adjutant General, Record Group 94, U. S. Army Hospital Department Registers, Vols. 50 and 52, Fort Stanton and Fort Sumner, 1862-67.

Records of the Office of Quartermaster General, Record Group 92, Consolidated Correspondence File Relating to Fort Sumner.

Records of U. S. Army Commands, Department of New Mexico, Record Group 98, Letters Received, 1860-70.

New Mexico Superintendency of Indian Affairs Papers, Record Group 75, Letters Received, 1860-1880.

New Mexico Superintendency of Indian Affairs, Record Group 75, Letters Sent, 1860-80.

U. S. Signal Corps, Photographic Collections, Fort Sumner, Fort Canby.

U. S. National Archives, State Department Record Division

State Department Territorial Papers, New Mexico, 1860-1870.

OTHER ARCHIVAL COLLECTIONS

Haile, Berard. Collection of Ethnologic Notes pertaining to the Navajo Indians, University of Arizona, Special Collections Department, Tucson.

Hayden, Carl. Biographical Collection of Arizona Pioneers, Arizona Pioneers' Historical Society, Tucson.

Holliday Collection, Arizona Pioneers' Historical Society, Tucson.

Munk Collection, Southwest Museum, Highland Park, California.

Navajo Land Claims Files, Land Claims Office, Navajo Tribe, Window Rock, Arizona.

Pioneers' Biographical Collection, Arizona Pioneers' Historical Society, Tucson.

Ritch, William G. Collection, Huntington Library, San Marino, California.

Van Valkenburgh, Richard. Collection of Ethnological and Historical Notes, Arizona Pioneers' Historical Society, Tucson.

NEWSPAPERS

Albuquerque *Rio Abajo Weekly Press,* 1863-64.
San Francisco *Alta California,* 1860-70.
Santa Fe *Weekly Gazette,* 1860-68.
Santa Fe *Weekly New Mexican,* 1860-68.

DIRECTORIES, REPORTS, LETTERS, DIARIES, ETC.

Abel, Annie H. (comp. & ed.). *The Official Correspondence of James S. Calhoun While Indian Agent at Santa Fe and Superintendent of Indian Affairs in New Mexico.* Washington: 1915.

————. (ed.). "Indian Affairs in New Mexico Under the Administration of William Carr Lane. From the Journal of John Ward," *New Mexico Historical Review.* April & July 1941.

Abert, J. W. *Report of Lt. J. W. Abert, of his Examination of New Mexico, in the Years 1846-47.* Washington: 1848.

Annual Report of Commissioners of Indian Affairs, 1860-70. Washington.

Appleton's Cyclopaedia of American Biography. New York: 1899-1900, 6 vols.

Backus, Maj. Electus. "An Account of the Navajoes of New Mexico," *Indian Tribes of the United States,* edited by Henry Schoolcraft. Philadelphia: Lippincott, 1856, Vol. IV.

Bailey, L. R. *The Navajo Reconnaissance.* Los Angeles: Westernlore Press, 1964.

Bennett, James A. *Forts and Forays or A Dragoon in New Mexico,* edited by C. E. Brooks and F. D. Reeve. Albuquerque, University of New Mexico Press, 1948.

Bibo, Nathan. "Reminiscences of Early Days in New Mexico," Albuquerque *Evening Herald,* June 11, 1922.

Cremony, John C. *Life Among the Apaches.* San Francisco: 1868.

Cullum, George W. *Biographical Register of the Officers and Graduates of the U. S. Military Academy.* Boston and New York: 1891, 2 vols.

Davis, W. W. H. *El Gringo: Or New Mexico and Her People.* Santa Fe: Rydal Press, 1938.

Dictionary of American Biography. New York: 1928-44, 20 vols.

Gregory, Herbert E. *The Navajo Country, a Geographic and Hydrographic Reconnaissance of Parts of Arizona, New Mexico and Utah.* Washington: 1916.

Gwyther, George A. "An Indian Reservation," *Overland Monthly.* Vol X, January 1873.

Heitman, F. B. *Historical Register of the United States Army.* Washington: 1890, 3 vols.

Hodge, Frederick W. *Handbook of American Indians North of Mexico.* New York: Pageant Books, 1960, 2 vols.

Lindgren, Raymond E. (ed.). "A Diary of Kit Carson's Navaho Campaign, 1863-1864," *New Mexico Historical Review.* Vol. XXI, July 1946.

Meline, James F. *Two Thousand Miles on Horseback.* New York: American News Co., 1873.

Marino, C. C. "The Ceboyetanos and the Navahos," *New Mexico Historical Review.* Vol XXIX, January 1954.

"Reminiscences of Fort Defiance, New Mexico, 1860," *Journal of the Military Service Institution of the U. S.* Vol IV, 1883.

Royce, Charles C. (comp.). "Indian Land Cessions in the United States," *18th Annual Report of the Bureau of American Ethnology.* Washington: 1897, Part II.

Simpson, James H. *Journal of a Military Reconnaissance, from Santa Fe to the Navajo Country.* Philadelphia: Lippincott, Grambo & Co., 1852.

U. S. Army. *Revised Regulations.* Washington: 1863.

U. S. *Congressional Globe.* Washington: 1866-67,

U. S. 38th Congress, 1st Session, *House Executive Document.* No. 70.

U. S. 40th Congress, 2nd Session, *House Executive Document.* Vol. XIX.

U. S. 40th Congress, 2nd Session, *House Executive Documents.* Nos. 97, 185, 248 and 308.

U. S. Joint Special Committee on Indian Affairs. *Condition of the Tribes.* Washington: 1867.

U. S. 36th Congress, 1st Session, *Senate Executive Document.* Vol. II, Part II.

U. S. 40th Congress, 1st Session, *Senate Executive Document.* Vol. XII.

War of the Rebellion: Official Records of the Union and Confederate Armies. Washington: 1891-96.

BOOKS, MONOGRAPHS, ARTICLES, ETC.

Amsden, Charles. "The Navaho Exile at Bosque Redondo," *New Mexico Historical Review.* Vol. VIII, January 1933.

Arrott, James W. *A Brief History of Fort Union.* Las Vegas: New Mexico Highlands University, 1962.

Bailey, L. R. *The Long Walk.* Pasadena: Socio-Technical Books, 1970.

————. "The Captive Wars: Slave Taking as a Source of the Navajo Wars, 1846-68," *The Brand Book*. Los Angeles: Corral of Westerners, 1963.

Bancroft, Hubert H. *History of Arizona and New Mexico*. San Francisco: The History Co., 1890.

Dale, Edward E. *The Indians of the Southwest*. Norman: University of Oklahoma, 1949.

Dunn, J. P. *Massacres of the Mountains: A History of the Indian Wars of the Far West*. New York: Harpers, 1886.

Franciscan Fathers. *An Ethnologic Dictionary of the Navaho Language*. Saint Michaels: 1910.

Haile, Berard. "Navaho Chantways and Ceremonials," *American Anthropologist*. October-December 1938.

Hill, W. W. "Navaho Warfare," *Yale University Publications in Anthropology*. New Haven, 1936, No. V.

————. "Some Aspects of Navajo Political Structure," *Plateau*, Vol. XIII, No. 2.

————. *The Agricultural and Hunting Methods of the Navajo Indians*. New Haven: Yale University Press, 1938.

Hunt, Aurora. *Major General James H. Carleton*. Glendale: Arthur H. Clark Co., 1958.

Keleher, William A. *Turmoil in New Mexico*. Santa Fe: Rydal Press, 1951.

Kerby, Robert L. *The Confederate Invasion of New Mexico and Arizona*. Los Angeles: Westernlore Press, 1958.

Kluckhohn, Clyde. *Navaho Witchcraft*. Boston: Beacon Press, 1944.

Kluckhohn, Clyde and Dorothea Leighton. *The Navaho*. Cambridge: Harvard University Press, 1946.

Leighton, Alexander H., *The Governing of Men*. New York: Octagon Books, Inc., 1964.

Lipps, Oscar H. *The Navajos.* Cedar Rapids: Torch Press, 1909.

Luomala, Katharine. *Navaho Life Yesterday and Today.* Berkeley: Department of Interior, 1938.

McNitt, Frank. *The Indian Traders.* Norman: University of Oklahoma Press, 1962.

Mangiante, Rosal. *History of Fort Defiance.* Unpublished thesis, University of Arizona, Tucson, 1950.

Reeve, Frank C. "Federal Indian Policy in New Mexico, 1858-80," *New Mexico Historical Review.* Vol. XII, July 1937.

Reichard, Gladys A. *Social Life of the Navajo Indians.* New York: Columbia University Press, 1929.

Rister, C. C. "Harmful Practices of Indian Traders of the Southwest, 1865-1876," *New Mexico Historical Review.* Vol. VI, July 1931.

Sabin, Edwin L. *Kit Carson Days: Adventures in the Path of Empire.* New York: 1935.

Sapir, Edward and Hoijer, Harry (eds.). *Navaho Texts.* Iowa City: Linquistic Society of America, 1942.

Twitchell, Ralph E. *The Leading Facts of New Mexican History.* Cedar Rapids: Torch Press, 1912. 2 vols.

Underhill, Ruth. *Here Come the Navaho.* Washington: Indian Service, 1953.

Van Valkenburgh, Richard. *Diné Bikéyah.* Window Rock: Department of Interior, 1941.

————. "Navajo Naataani," *The Kiva.* Vol. XIII, January 1948.

Waldrip, William I. "New Mexico During the Civil War," *New Mexico Historical Review.* Vol. XXVIII, July 1953 and October 1953.

Index

Index

The text of this book is set in Linotype Caledonia, and printed by hand, on a special designed press possessing a monitored inking system to insure uniformity and strength of the printed image.